Kobe University Monograph Series in Social Science Research

The Kobe University Monograph Series in Social Science Research is an exciting interdisciplinary collection of monographs, both authored and edited, that encompass scholarly research not only in the economics but also in law, political science, business and management, accounting, international relations, and other sub-disciplines within the social sciences. As a national university with a special strength in the social sciences, Kobe University actively promotes interdisciplinary research. This series is not limited only to research emerging from Kobe University's faculties of social sciences but also welcomes cross-disciplinary research that integrates studies in the arts and sciences.

Kobe University, founded in 1902, is the second oldest national higher education institution for commerce in Japan and is now a preeminent institution for social science research and education in the country. Currently, the social sciences section includes four faculties—Law, Economics, Business Administration, and International Cooperation Studies—and the Research Institute for Economics and Business Administration (RIEB). There are some 230-plus researchers who belong to these faculties and conduct joint research through the Center for Social Systems Innovation and the Organization for Advanced and Integrated Research, Kobe University. This book series comprises academic works by researchers in the social sciences at Kobe University as well as their collaborators at affiliated institutions, Kobe University alumni and their colleagues, and renowned scholars from around the world who have worked with academic staff at Kobe University. Although traditionally the research of Japanese scholars has been publicized mainly in the Japanese language, Kobe University strives to promote publication and dissemination of works in English in order to further contribute to the global academic community.

More information about this series at http://www.springer.com/series/16115

Masahiko Yoshii · Chae-Deug Yi
Editors

An Economic Analysis of Korea–EU FTA and Japan–EU EPA

Editors
Masahiko Yoshii
Graduate School of Economics
Kobe University
Kobe, Hyogo, Japan

Chae-Deug Yi
College of Economics and International
Trade
Pusan National University
Busan, Republic of Korea

ISSN 2524-504X   ISSN 2524-5058   (electronic)
Kobe University Monograph Series in Social Science Research
ISBN 978-981-33-6144-7   ISBN 978-981-33-6145-4   (eBook)
https://doi.org/10.1007/978-981-33-6145-4

This Springer imprint is published by the registered company Springer Nature Singapore Pte Ltd.
The registered company address is: 152 Beach Road, #21-01/04 Gateway East, Singapore 189721, Singapore

The original version of this book was revised: Book Editor (Chae-Deug Yi) affiliation and chapter 3 corrections has been updated. The correction to this book can be found at https://doi.org/10.1007/978-981-33-6145-4_7

Contents

About the Editors

Masahiko Yoshii is a professor of economics and currently serves as Executive Vice President in charge of international exchange and university evaluation at Kobe University. He joined the Faculty of Economics there in 1985, and was promoted to full professor in 1998. He was the dean of the Graduate School of Economics at Kobe University in the years 2012–2014. He also has worked at the Embassy of Japan in Bucharest, Romania 1990–1992 and was a visiting researcher at the Vienna Institute of International Economic Studies (WiiW) 2001–2002. He was appointed as a Jean Monnet Chair for 2015–2018 and now serves as a coordinator of the Jean Monnet Centre of Excellence at Kobe University.

Dr. Yoshii's major research interests are comparative economic systems and the economies of Central and Eastern European countries and Russia. He is also interested in the economic relationship between Japan and the EU. He is a member of the Japan Association of Russian and Eastern European Studies, the Japan Association of Comparative Economic Studies, the European Studies Association Japan, and the Japan Economic Policy Association, all of which associations he has served as a board member.

Professor Yoshii has many papers and books to his credit, including, as co-editor, *The EU in Turmoil* (Inoue and Yoshii, eds., Keiso-shobo, 2018); *Japan and the European Union in the Global Economy* (Guntram and Yoshii, eds., Bruegel Blueprint No. 22, 2014); *Deepening and Enlargement of the EU Integration and the Euro Crisis* (Kubo and Yoshii, eds., Keiso Shobo, 2013); and *Contemporary Russian Economy* (Mizobata and Yoshii, eds., Minerva 2011).

Chae-Deug Yi is a professor at the College of Economics and International Trade at Pusan National University (PNU), Republic of Korea. He received his Ph.D. in economics from Ohio State University, USA. He has worked as the founding director of the PNU EU Centre since 2009 and has been a Jean Monnet Chair holder in EU integration since 2010. He initiated and founded the ASIA—EU graduate student conference with Prof. Toshiro Tanaka (Keio University, Japan) in 2010. He has been teaching international trade and finance, econometrics, and EU economics at the Graduate School of International Studies, Law School, and College of Economics and International Trade, PNU, in Korea. He is now the president of the Korea Research

Association of International Commerce. He held visiting professional positions in the USA at Duke University 2005–2006 and at UC Berkeley 2015–2016, and in China at Yeonbin University of Science of Technology in 2002. He also attended the International Negotiation Project, Harvard University, USA, 1997, and the Econometrics Summer Camp, Cambridge University, UK, 2019.

Dr. Yi participated in the World Jean Monnet Conference and World EU Centre Conference in Madrid, Spain, in 2010 and made a presentation on the Korea–EU FTA in Belgium. He was invited to the National Taiwan University and Ministry of Foreign Affairs of the Government of Taiwan to advise the EU–Taiwan ECA agreement. He was also invited to several international EU conferences as a speaker or discussant in Brussels, Madrid, Keio, and Kobe universities (Japan), Irkutsk (Russia), Macao, Christ Church (NZ), Melbourne, Singapore, Taiwan, and Fudan University and Lenmin University (China), among others. He has published several books, including those on international commerce (1999), principles of international trade (2001), and international economics (2005). In addition, he has published more than 115 articles in leading Korean and international journals.

Chapter 1
Introduction

Masahiko Yoshii and Chae-Deug Yi

The world trade system after the World War II was sustained by the multi-national negotiation system whose core institution was the GATT/WTO. The basic principles of the GATT/WTO system were:

- Non-discrimination,
- Reciprocity,
- Binding and enforceable commitments,
- Transparency, and,
- Safety values.

Based on these principles the GATT/WTO organised a series of negotiation rounds to gradually reduce custom tariffs among the contracting countries, like Kennedy, Tokyo and Uruguay rounds.

However, since the 1990s, especially since the WTO's Doha Round which was officially launched in 2001 became locked in a stalemate, the contracting countries have focused to conclude bilateral free trade agreements (FTAs), instead of insisting on the GATT/WTO multilateral negotiation system. Today the number of FTAs in force in the world exceeds 300, though most of them were concluded in the 2000s.

The European Union (EU), Korea and Japan along with the United States are main actors in negotiating FTAs or regional trade agreements (RTAs), because of their strong economic power.

M. Yoshii (✉)
Graduate School of Economics, Kobe University, Kobe, Japan
e-mail: yoshii@kobe-u.ac.jp

C.-D. Yi
College of Economics and International Trade, Pusan National University, Busan, Republic of Korea
e-mail: givethanks@pusan.ac.kr

© Kobe University 2021

M. Yoshii and C.-D. Yi (eds.), *An Economic Analysis of Korea–EU FTA and Japan–EU EPA*, Kobe University Monograph Series in Social Science Research, https://doi.org/10.1007/978-981-33-6145-4_1

The EU is one of the biggest economy comparable to the U.S., even after the U.K. exited out of it. The EU itself has been a free trade area since 1958 when the original six member countries established the customs union, where customs duties in its bilateral trade are eliminated, and a joint customs tariff for foreign importers is established. Not only the EU enlarged the custom union area by increasing the member countries and by concluding FTAs with European non-member countries like Switzerland and Norway, but also it concluded FTAs at an early stage especially with former colony countries and other neighboring European countries hoping to be member countries in the future. Recently the EU concluded comprehensive trade agreements with Canada, Korea, Japan and other developed and developing countries as a vehicle to promote world trade in accordance with European values and norms.

Korea is a country with best economic performance among NIEs (Newly Industrialising Countries). Its exports of machinery and transport equipment, chemical products, and other manufacturing products have increased in a spectacular manner since the 2000s, especially since the global financial crisis in 2009. To increase further its exports to the developed countries, Korea actively uses FTA. Korea began FTA negotiations with the U.S. in 2006, and successfully concluded it in 2007, though the agreement entered into force finally in 2012, because of the delay of ratification by the U.S. side. And, Korea successfully continued to conclude FTA with the EU. Its negotiation started in 2007. The agreement was signed in 2009, provisionally applied in 2011, and entered into force in 2015. However, Korea could not have reached to conclude any bilateral FTA with Japan, though both are signatory countries of the RCEP (Regional Comprehensive Economic Partnership) which was signed in November 2020 by 15 Asia-Pacific countries including Korea and Japan.

Japan was very hesitant in the bilateral FTA at an early stage. The first was FTA/economic partnership agreement (EPA) with Singapore, which was concluded in 2002. The reasons were:

- Japan insisted on the WTO multilateral negotiation system,
- Farmers in Japan raised fierce opposition against reducing custom tariffs of imported agricultural products, and,
- Custom tariffs on industrial products had already been lifted or reduced to almost zero, because of severe trade conflicts with the U.S. and the EU.

However, soon after Korea began to negotiate FTAs with advanced countries in the beginning of the 2000s, the Japanese business circle raised a voice to the government for a more positive attitude to conclude FTAs/EPAs. Then, Japanese government decided to join the TPP (Trans-Pacific Partnership Agreement) negotiation in 2010, and, as we will see in this monograph, started the EPA negotiation with the EU in 2013.

This monograph tries to compare two FTAs among these three economic regions, that is, the Korea–EU FTA and the Japan–EU EPA. These FTAs/EPAs have several common characteristics. The first one is that, of course, a partner of these agreements is the EU, and the others are two economic superpowers in East Asia. Thus, similar goods are expected to be traded among, on the one hand, Korea and Japan, and, on the other hand, the EU, because of which the both sides may ask similar demands to the other side. The second one is that both FTAs entered into force very recently, that is, in the 2010, which makes comparison of recent results of the FTAs to be more interesting. The last one is that both FTAs/EPAs are comprehensive FTA agreements, containing not only tariff and non-tariff reductions but also other economic and social dimensions. Especially, comparing how Korea and Japan react to demands from the EU should inspire the academic interests.

Chapter 1 emphasises that, looking into the EU FTA and trade polic after the early 2000s, the EU's trade policy attaches special importance to social and political issues as well as to trade matters. The Korea–EU FTA is the EU's most 'comprehensive' and 'ambitious' new-generation FTA, as its 'Trade and Sustainable Development' chapter contained both labour and environmental standards. In the case of the Japan–EU EPA, it includes EU standards and values into chapters. For example, it respects sustainable development, especially higher levels of labour and environmental protection, as a key concept.

Chapter 2 empirically studies the Korea–EU FTA. First, it summarises the general trend and structures of trades between Korea and the EU, and shows Korea's comparative advantage indices to express that Korea has highest comparative advantages in such manufacturing industries as motor vehicles, electrical machinery and equipment and parts, and boats. Next, it simulates the economic effects of the Korea–EU FTA on Korea, Japan, the EU and the rest of the world by using the CGE model. The results confirm positive impacts of the Korea–EU FTA on the bilateral trade and their GDP.

Chapter 3 gives a general description of the Japan–EU EPA. After looking into the past and today of the bilateral trade, it explains what was negotiated and what was concluded. The general level of tariff elimination is close to that of the Trans–Pacific Partnership Agreement (TPP) 11, but also adopted various non–tariff measures as well as tariff measures on traded goods and services to upgrade the bilateral economic relationships.

Chapter 4 simulates economic effects of the Japan–EU EPA and Brexit by using the inter-country input–output table. First, the simulation shows that the Japan–EU EPA will decrease price levels both in the EU and in Japan, with different impacts on sectors and countries. Next, impacts of hard Brexit are estimated. If the U.K. fails in concluding any trade agreements with the EU and Japan, both sides' trade costs will increase and international competitiveness of the U.K. will be lower.

Chapter 5 analyses results of the questionnaire held by the author himself to show how Japanese small and medium enterprises evaluate the Japan–EU EPA. It concludes that because the EU markets still account for a small proportion of their total revenue, Japanese small and medium enterprises expect the EU market to give them an opportunity to grow and become more internationalized.

Through these analyses we expect to show that both the Korea–EU FTA and the Japan–EU EPA will not only create more favorable trade and economic conditions in these countries but also give spillover effects to create more comprehensive, including social and political, conditions in other Asian countries. Of course, it is too early to make a decisive conclusion, because, first, only one year has passed since the Japan–EU EPA came into effect, and, second, the global economy faces "once in a century" crisis because of the COVIT-19 spread.

This monograph is a result of joint research "Japan–Korea Economic Cooperation through Comparative Analysis on Japan–EU EPA/FTA and Korea–EU FTA" supported by the Japan Society for the Promotion of Science and the National Research Foundation of Korea Bilateral Joint Projects scheme in 2018–2019. We appreciate for precious financial assistance by both institutions. Most of researchers involved in the project have been core members of the Pusan National University EU Centre/Jean Monnet Centre of Excellence, PNU, and the EU Institute in Japan, Kansai/Kobe University Jean Monnet Centre of Excellence, all supported by the European Commission since the middle of 2000s, and have communicated for more than a decade. However, without the financial assistance of NRF and JSPS this monograph could not been compiled. We hope this cooperation would continue, and further contribute to deepen the level of research on the economic relationships between Japan and Korea, on the one hand, and the EU, on the other hand.

Chapter 2
The EU-Korea Free Trade Agreement Versus the EU-Japan Economic Partnership Agreement

Hiromasa Kubo

Abstract The European Union's free trade agreement has recently changed to impact a new generation, with a greater emphasis on the European Union's values. Reflecting this, the free trade agreement between the European Union and Korea became effective in December 2015, with a 'trade and sustainable development' chapter. Similarly, the economic partnership agreement between the European Union and Japan has a similar section, but with further detail. The parties in these chapters agreed to reaffirm the importance of free trade and the relationships between free trade and climate, as well as workers' rights. The European Commission considered the free trade agreement between the European Union and Korea in calling for government consultations on workers' rights with Korea. While it is still early, the Commission may require similar consultations with Japan. When we observe the recent changes in world trade, protectionist movements are becoming increasingly popular; therefore, it is noteworthy that the economic partnership agreement between the European Union and Japan—which is considered a 'mega' free trade agreement—should appealing benefits from such free trades in spite of their value to the European Union.

Keywords Economic partnership agreement · Free trade agreement · Trade and sustainable development

2.1 Introduction

The economic partnership agreement (EPA) between the European Union (EU) and Japan took effect in February 2019, more than three years after the EU-Korea free trade agreement (FTA). During these three years, the EU's FTA and trade policy changed significantly to reach a new generation. This paper will first review the EU's

H. Kubo (✉)
Faculty of Economics, Setsunan University, 17-8 Ikedanaka-machi,
Neyagawa 572-8508, Osaka, Japan
e-mail: h-kubo@econ.setsunan.ac.jp

© Kobe University 2021
M. Yoshii and C.-D. Yi (eds.), *An Economic Analysis of Korea–EU FTA and Japan–EU EPA*, Kobe University Monograph Series in Social Science Research,
https://doi.org/10.1007/978-981-33-6145-4_2

policy, then summarise the FTA and EPA, respectively. Finally, we will examine these two agreements' effects on their respective economies.

2.2 A 'Global Europe'

Since the European Coal and Steel Community was established in 1952, Europe has moved towards a customs union, which was formed by the 1968 Treaty of Rome. A customs union is a type of regional trade agreement that sets common tariffs outside a region while eliminating tariff barriers within the region. On the one hand, the European Union (EU) has consistently established its own regional trade agreements from the beginning; on the other hand, it has also focused on strengthening a multilateral trade system under the General Agreement on Tariffs and Trade (GATT) and the World Trade Organisation (WTO). However, the EU's FTA has long been used for various purposes. For example, the EU's FTA was sometimes used to address political and diplomatic issues—such as preparing for EU membership or promoting economic development in former colonies of EU member states—rather than exploiting the economic benefits of removing trade barriers.[1]

The international economic environment surrounding the EU has significantly changed since the early 2000s due to the rise of the original BRICs nations, or specifically, Brazil, Russia, India, and China, and the activation of the United States' FTA, called the 'competitive liberalisation' strategy.[2] Additionally, while the EU made considerable strides in the WTO's Doha Round negotiations, they ultimately became locked in a stalemate due to conflicts, whether among developed countries or between developed and developing countries.[3] Under such circumstances, the European Commission published a communication in October 2006 entitled 'Global Europe: Competing in the World'.[4] This aimed to define FTAs as one method to pursue economic profits by strengthening the international competitiveness of European industries while still maintaining the EU's respect for multilateralism through the WTO. 'Global Europe' also emphasized the importance of abolishing the customs barrier as well as non-tariff barriers (NTBs) through such initiatives as harmonising intellectual property rights, competition policies, and government procurements, which were difficult to achieve in international and multilateral negotiations. Moreover, the report selected target areas based on various criteria, including the economic scale, growth potential, and levels of trade barriers, to conclude FTAs with other countries. In particular, the targeted regions and countries included the Association of Southeast Asian Nations, Korea, and the *Mercado Común del Sur*. This report also highlighted China, India, Russia, and the Gulf Cooperation Council as candidate countries, although it did not mention Japan. After 'Global Europe' was

---

[1] Woolcock [21].
[2] Simon [20].
[3] Daniel and Marc [3].
[4] European Commission [8].

published, the EU began its FTA negotiations with these regions. Consequently, the EU also began its FTA negotiations with Korea in May 2007, and they were fully implemented in December 2015.

The European Commission published a new communication—'Trade, Growth and World Affairs: Trade Policy as a Core Component of the EU's 2020 Strategy'—in November 2010.[5] This externally supported the EU's economic growth strategies that were adopted in March of the same year; such strategies include three pillars from the communication's 'Europe 2020' focus: smart, sustainable, and inclusive growth.[6] To achieve these aims, the communication emphasized the importance of reducing NTBs and liberalising and harmonising government procurements, among other processes. Further, it regarded the United States, China, Japan, and Canada as strategic trade partners and underscored efforts to strengthen their trade relationships.

The EU began its Transatlantic Trade and Investment Partnership (TTIP) negotiations with the United States in July 2013,[7] after 'Trade, Growth and World Affairs' was published. However, EU civil societies and nongovernmental and non-profit organisations expressed their criticism with (1) omitting the GATT general exception for regulatory purposes (Article XX); (2) omitting the issue of climate protections; (3) abandoning the precautionary principle; and (4) allowing corporate lobbies to influence trade negotiations.[8] Although the EU-Korea FTA had been provisionally applied since July 2011 before its formal ratification in December 2015, EU experts were anxious that the EU's exports to Korea were not remarkable, which raised doubts about the FTA's effectiveness. In fact, the EU's share of exports to Korea to its total exports was 2.1% in 2012, compared with 1.9% in 2008. The European Commission addressed these various but significant issues surrounding the EU's FTA and trade policy by proposing a new trade and investment strategy for the European Union in October 2015, entitled 'Trade for All: Towards a More Responsible Trade and Investment Policy'.[9]

2.3 'Trade for All: Towards a more Responsible Trade and Investment Policy'

The EU's 'Trade for All' publication aimed to strengthen the region's competitive advantage by focusing more on such areas as services and digital trade. It also aimed to strengthen the provision of information to small and medium-sized enterprises to promote effective utilisation. In response to concerns from civil societies raised during the TTIP negotiation process, this publication also emphasized further

---

[5]European Commission [11].

[6]European Commission [10].

[7]European Commission [4].

[8]European Parliament [5].

[9]European Commission [12].

dialogue regarding trade negotiations with member states, the European Parliament, and civil societies, including labour unions, to increase transparency in the negotiation process.

'Trade for All' also highlighted the need for consistency to align trade strategies with the EU's values, such as democracy, respect for human rights, and the rule of law. Further, such values would be reflected in the trade agreement deals and issues that the EU determined were of importance, such as sustainable development and eliminating both child labour and corruption. Therefore, it could be said that the EU's FTA policy has reached a more comprehensive evolution in covering trade matters as well as social and political issues.

Consequently, the Investor-State Dispute Settlement (ISDS) clause was a key issue in TTIP negotiations, as there were concerns that it might cause significant problems given the uncertainty in the arbitration process and the unpredictability of arbitration decisions while recognising the importance of investor protections.[10] One important issue in future trade agreements involves the establishing of a permanent investment court. In the EU-Korea FTA and EU-Japan EPA, agreements have been reached to separate negotiations of each agreement and the ISDS.

In this brief history of the EU's FTA and trade policy, we observe two developments in the EU that affected this policy. The first is the Treaty of Lisbon,[11] which took effect in December 2009 and expanded the European Parliament's power. A co-decision procedure with the Council on trade-related matters has been applied; approval from the European Parliament is required and it must ratify all trade agreements. Therefore, the European Commission must regularly report on the progress of trade negotiations to the European Council as well as the European Parliament. In other words, the European Parliament's increased involvement in trade agreement negotiations significantly strengthened a 'visualisation' of the negotiation process, and thus, more 'transparent' negotiations were also required.

Consequently, civil societies have become important in the EU's trade strategy and negotiation approach. In summary, due to the Lisbon Treaty, the agreement of the European Parliament is required to ratify; thus, the Commission must report any negotiation processes to the European Parliament and civil societies—such as the European Economic and Social Committee—even at initial negotiation stages. Therefore, the European Parliament is typically important in implementing FTAs under this legal framework.

The second important development impacting the EU's FTA policy is the opinion of the European Court of Justice. For example, the EU-Singapore FTA is based on the European Court of Justice's May 2017 opinion regarding the allocation of authority between the EU and its member states.[12] The EU-Singapore as well as the EU-Vietnam FTAs—which are characterised as new-generation FTAs—present separate investment-protection agreements. Other FTA agreements should be regarded as 'mixed agreements' that require ratification by both the European Parliament and

---

[10]European Commission, *op. cit.* (7).

[11]Official Journal of the European Union [15].

[12]European Commission [9].

all member states. As a result of the European Court of Justice's opinion, the EU's FTAs are currently composed of only areas with exclusive authority; as no element of authority is shared with member states, it is possible for such FTAs to take effect early, rather than come into effect only provisionally.

It is also noteworthy that before such an opinion, both the EU and its member states signed an FTA with Canada (CETA) in July 2016, or specifically, a mixed agreement in response to requests from Germany and France. On 14 October in the same year, the Belgian Walloon Parliament opposed the signing of an FTA with Canada. As Belgium has a federal system, the central government needs the local parliament's consent to ratify international agreements; thus, the Belgian government cannot sign if the local parliament opposes the signature. However, the Wallonia Parliament ultimately accepted the Agreement, and it was enacted in September 2017.[13]

2.4   The EU-Korea Free Trade Agreement

Korea highly depends on trade, and has made considerable strategic efforts to conclude FTAs with other countries or regions since 2003 with the aim of promoting foreign trades. Specifically, they have targeted large economic and/or resource-rich countries.[14] As of January 2018, Korea had FTAs with 52 countries worldwide. However, at the beginning of the 2000s, Korea was behind Japan in promoting its FTAs; in fact, Korea's first FTA came into force with Chile in 2004, while Japan made its first EPA with Singapore in 2002.

After eight rounds of negotiations beginning in May 2007, the EU-Korea FTA was provisionally applied in July 2011, although European auto industry groups and even the European Parliament presented opposition. The FTA became effective in December 2015 after having been ratified by all signatories.[15]

Due to this Agreement, Korea's second export destination after China is the EU, which will eliminate customs duties within five years. Specifically, the EU still maintains high tariffs, such as for electrical equipment and electronics (up to 14%) and passenger cars (up to 10%), while Korean manufacturers will no longer be burdened with such customs duties. This is not only the EU's first FTA in Asia, but also has symbolic significance as the first comprehensive and advanced FTA, as previously discussed, regarding the 2006 'Global Europe' initiative. Additionally, Korea's tariffs, NTBs, and service barriers will be removed, among other limitations (see Table 2.1).

Generally, Korea will immediately eliminate 82% of its tariffs, and 94% of the EU's tariffs will also be removed. In five years, 94 and 99.6% of Korea's and the EU's tariffs will be eliminated, respectively, with the EU and Korea both eliminating

---

[13]CBC News [1].

[14]Cheong [2].

[15]Official Journal of the European Union [16].

Table 2.1 Chapters in "the EU-Korea free trade agreement"

Chapter 1	Objectives and general definitions
Chapter 2	National treatment and market access for goods
Chapter 3	Anti-Dumping and countervailing duties
Chapter 4	Technical barriers to trade
Chapter 5	Sanitary and phytosanitary measures
Chapter 6	Customs and trade facilitation
Chapter 7	Trade in services, establishment and electronic commerce
Chapter 8	Payments and capital movements
Chapter 9	Government procurement
Chapter 10	Intellectual property
Chapter 11	Competition
Chapter 12	Transparency
Chapter 13	Trade and sustainable development
Chapter 14	Dispute settlement
Chapter 15	Institutional, general and final provisions

Source Official journal of the European union [16]

at least 98% of their tariffs in seven years. Further, the Agreement will eliminate 94.5% of Korean tariffs in 3 years, with virtually all tariffs eliminated in 10 years.

Therefore, the FTA not only has high-level content for reducing tariffs but also covers a broad range of NTBs, services, liberalisation and harmonisation processes, and intellectual property rights, among other factors. This is even clearer than in the EU's FTAs thus far. In the FTAs signed by the EU before 'Global Europe', the degree of liberalisation among agricultural products was substantially low—such as in the EU-Chile and EU-Mexico FTAs—or separate negotiations occurred regarding the liberalisation of agricultural products. However, the EU-Korea FTA even covers agricultural products, and includes a focus on trade and sustainable development (Chapter 13) that defines environmental and worker protections by considering the requirements of the European Parliament and civil societies.[16]

However, the content of tariff reductions in the EU's FTA with Korea is nearly the same as in the US-Korea FTA, and the government's explanation emphasized this fact. Agricultural products, and rice in particular, were treated as exceptional, and generally are less liberalised than in the US-Korea FTA. Moreover, NTB rules and intellectual property rights, and especially geographical indications and subsidy regulations, among others, are essentially the same as those in the U.S. and Korea.

As previously discussed, the EU-Korea FTA was the EU's most 'comprehensive' and 'ambitious' new-generation FTA, as its 'Trade and Sustainable Development' chapter contained both labour and environmental standards. This FTA states that 'the Parties (the EU and Korea) reaffirm their commitments to promoting the development

---

[16]Pardo et al. [18].

of international trade in such a way as to contribute to the objective of sustainable development and will strive to ensure that this objective is integrated and reflected at every level of their trade relations' (Chapter 13.1) and 'the Parties reaffirm the commitment to effectively implementing the ILO (International Labour Organisation) Conventions that Korea and the Member States of the European Union have ratified respectively' (Chapter 13.4).

Chapter 13.13 involves establishing a Civil Society Forum as an institutional framework to facilitate a dialogue on the sustainable development aspects of trade relations between the parties. However, it is often reported that workers' rights in Korea are restricted, such as their 'freedom of association'. Although the Commission's assessment of a five-year post-implementation period concluded that 'the EU-Korea FTA was effective in promoting trade between the European Union and Korea',[17] Chapter 13 is one of the most problematic points.

2.5 The Japan-EU Economic Partnership Agreement

2.5.1 Outlines of the EPA

The EU-Japan EPA[18] was implemented in February 2019 with the EU-Japan Strategic Partnership Agreement,[19] which promoted political cooperation between the EU and Japan. The former agreement aimed to promote free trade as protectionist movements spread worldwide, such as the United Kingdom's move towards leaving the EU and the United States' withdrawal from the Trans-Pacific Partnership Agreement,[20] based on President Trump's 'America First' position. As a mega-FTA, its impact on the global economy—and thus, the international economic order—has drawn significant attention.[21]

Generally, the EU-Japan EPA regulates the same level of liberalisation and comprehensive trade rules as the Trans-Pacific Partnership, as well as advanced regulations that can correspond to Japanese companies' economic activities and trade rules that are unmatched by other FTAs. However, strong concerns have been expressed regarding the EPA's impact on the domestic agricultural, forestry and fisheries industry due to the EU's expanded imports of such products.

Regarding exports from the EU to Japan, cheese currently has tariffs of 29.8% in principle, but will be phased out over the next 15 years, and wine (15% or 125 yen per litre) will be immediately eliminated. Tariffs on pasta, chocolate, and pork will

---

[17] European Commission [6].

[18] Ministry of Foreign Affairs of Japan [13].

[19] Ministry of Foreign Affairs of Japan, Strategic Partnership Agreement between the European Union and its Member States, of One Part and Japan, of the Other Part. https://www.mofa.go.jp/mofaj/files/000381942.pdf, accessed 21 Dec 2019.

[20] New Zealand Foreign Affairs and Trade [14].

[21] Shujiro Urata [19].

Table 2.2 Shares of the EU and Japan worldwide (in %)

	Population	GDP
EU	6.8	22.1
Japan	1.7	5.9
EU + Japan	8.5	28.0

Source World Bank, *World Development Indicators,* Oct 2019

be removed in 10 years, while those on leather products will be eliminated in 10 or 15 years. Cheese and pork account for a small percentage of total imports, but eliminating these tariffs will significantly impact domestic dairy and livestock industries; further, concerns exist regarding the impacts on producers. Regarding customs duties on exports from Japan to the EU, tariffs on automobiles as the largest export item (currently 10%) will be eliminated in seven years, and tariffs on approximately 90% of automotive parts (currently 3% to 4.5%) will be eliminated immediately. Tariffs on televisions will be abolished in five years, and those on sake, green tea, seasoning (soy sauce), fruits and vegetables and meat and dairy products will be abolished immediately. According to the Japanese government, the EPA has a wider scope of negotiations than a traditional FTA; in addition to trade, the EPA also includes regulations on finance and investments; information and communications; and such intellectual property as patents, trademarks and geographical indications.

In addition to bilateral trade relations, the EPA will recognise a substantial free trade zone, with a population of 635 million and approximately 30% of the world's gross domestic product (GDP), while simultaneously strengthening cooperation between the EU and Japan on a wide range of global issues (see Table 2.2). In addition to reaffirming each other's responsibility for sustainable developments, this FTA is the first to clearly state its responsibility in implementing the Paris Agreement on climate change. The agreement is primarily characterised by a comprehensive chapter on trade and sustainable development, and has high standards for labour, safety, environmental and consumer protections, among others. These standards also include strengthening commitments from both the EU and Japan in possible development and climate change measures, and in adequately protecting workers' rights.

2.5.2 Characteristics of the EPA

One characteristic of the EU-Japan EPA is the inclusion of EU standards and values. For example, the EU requested a provision on the protection of geographic indications. In response, Japan established a geographical labelling-protections system during negotiations to address this issue. Chapter 14 in the EPA is devoted to intellectual property rights. Specifically, Section B, paragraph 3 in this Chapter defines geographic indications to protect EU and Japanese regional specialties: for example, French Bordeaux wine; German Lübecker marzipan; Italian Gorgonzola cheese; and Japan's Yamanashi wine, Miwa noodles, and Kobe beef are listed as separate, protected foods and beverages.

Table 2.3 Chapters in "The EU-Japan economic partnership agreement"

Chapter 1	General provisions
Chapter 2	Trade in goods
Chapter 3	Rules of origin and origin procedures
Chapter 4	Customs matters and trade facilitation
Chapter 5	Trade remedies
Chapter 6	Sanitary and phytosanitary measures
Chapter 7	Technical barriers to trade
Chapter 8	Trade in services, investment liberalisation and electronic commerce
Chapter 9	Capital movements, payments and transfers and temporary safeguard measures
Chapter 10	Government procurement
Chapter 11	Competition policy
Chapter 12	Subsidies
Chapter 13	State-Owned enterprises, enterprises granted special rights or privileges, and designated monopolies
Chapter 14	Intellectual property
Chapter 15	Corporate governance
Chapter 16	Trade and sustainable development
Chapter 17	Transparency
Chapter 18	Good regulatory practices and regulatory cooperation
Chapter 19	Cooperation in the field of agriculture
Chapter 20	Small and medium-sized enterprises
Chapter 21	Dispute settlement
Chapter 22	Institutional provisions
Chapter 23	Final provisions

Source Ministry of foreign affairs of Japan [13]

The EPA also includes a chapter for trade and sustainable development (Chapter 16), as 'sustainable development' is a key concept in this Agreement (see Table 2.3). This has also been included in the Treaty of Lisbon, as 'it [the EU] shall work for the sustainable development of Europe' (Article 3.3), 'it shall contribute to peace, security, [and] the sustainable development of the Earth' (Article 3.5), and will 'preserve and improve the quality of the environment and the sustainable management of global natural resources, in order to ensure sustainable development' (Article 21.2, Section F).

The Treaty on the Functioning of the EU[22] provides similar stipulations, stating that 'environmental protection requirements must be integrated into the definition and implementation of the Union's policies and activities, in particular with a view to promoting sustainable development' (Article 11), and 'to promote good governance

---

[22]Official Journal of the European Union [17].

and ensure the participation of civil society, the Union's institutions, bodies, offices and agencies shall conduct their work as openly as possible' (Article 15.1).

The EU-Japan EPA also stipulates that 'the Parties [the EU and Japan] recognise the importance of promoting the development of international trade in a way that contributes to sustainable development, for the welfare of present and future generations, taking into consideration the Agenda 21 adopted by the United Nations Conference on Environment and Development on 14 June 1992, the ILO Declaration on Fundamental Principles and Rights at Work and its follow-up adopted by the International Labour Conference on 18 June 1998' (Article 16.1).

Further, Article 16.3 in the EPA states that 'the Parties recognise full and productive employment and decent work for all as key elements to respond to economic, labour and social challenges. The Parties further recognise the importance of promoting the development of international trade in a way that is conducive to full and productive employment and decent work for all'.

Therefore, the concept of sustainable development is reflected in this EPA not only in economic and environmental terms, but also from a social perspective given its focus on worker protections, as European nongovernmental organisations expressed concern that the EU would decrease its protection standards by signing an FTA with other countries outside the EU.

The EPA confirms that 'each Party shall strive to ensure that its laws, regulations and related policies provide high levels of environmental and labour protection and shall strive to continue to improve those laws and regulations and their underlying levels of protection' (Article 16.2). Further, 'the Parties reaffirm their obligations deriving from the International Labour Organisation membership (Article 16.3.2), and 'the Parties shall exchange information on their respective situations as regards the ratification of ILO Conventions and Protocols, including the fundamental ILO Conventions' (Article 16.3.4). If 'the Parties do not reach a mutually satisfactory resolution of the matter concerning the interpretation or application of the relevant Articles of this Chapter, a Party may request that a panel of experts be convened to examine the matter' (Article 16.18.1).

2.6 Conclusions

In December 2018, the European Commission began its 'government consultations' of the Korean government under the EU-Korea FTA (Chapter 13.14), as Korea's government had not yet ratified the ILO's core agreements.[23] This is the first time in its history that the EU has entered into a dispute-settlement procedure for labour rights provisions under a free trade agreement. Subsequently, the Commission repeated its requests for implementation, as 'the Parties reaffirm the commitment to effectively implementing the ILO Conventions that Korea and the Member States of the European Union have ratified respectively' (Chapter 13.5).

---

[23] European Commission [7].

According to the Agreement, if a compromise is not reached within 90 days, they can call a 'panel of experts' (Chapter 14.15) including at least 15 experts, of whom at least 5 are be non-nationals of either party (Article 13.15.3). Unless both parties agree, each will only have recourse regarding the dispute settlement procedures (Chapter 14).

The eight core agreements adopted by the ILO's General Assembly include workers' basic rights, such as the freedom of association, prohibition of forced or child labour, and the prohibition of discrimination. Korea has not yet ratified agreements on the 'freedom of association' (87 and 98) and the 'elimination of forced labour' (29 and 105).

It might be difficult to predict the final outcome of a consultation between the EU and Korea. However, we must consider that Japan has not yet ratified two of the ILO's eight core labour standard conventions: the prohibition of forced labour (No. 29 and No. 105) and the prohibition of discrimination (No. 110). Following Korea, the EU is likely to call Japan to a consultation under its EPA (Article 16).

As previously discussed, the EU's FTA policy has changed remarkably after the 'Trade for All' report. Consequently, the EU aims to not only exploit economic benefits, but also increase economic value throughout the EU. Therefore, the number of words in the 'trade and sustainable development' chapter has significantly increased, from some 2,300 words (Chapter 13 in the FTA) to approximately 5,000 words (Chapter 16 in the EPA).

However, recent global economic developments indicate that protectionism has become increasingly popular. If the EU adheres to its values in trade agreements, then a mega-FTA—such as the EU-Japan EPA—may reduce its ability to appeal to the importance of free trade worldwide. The world can carefully observe how the EU will manage both the EU-Korea Free Trade Agreement and the EU-Japan Economic Partnership Agreement.

References

1. CBC News. (2016). *Walloons Now Say Yes, as Canada-EU Trade Deal Clears Final Votes*. Retrieved December 21, 2019, from https://www.cbc.ca/news/politics/canada-eu-trade-friday-votes-1.3825583.
2. Cheong, I. (2014). *Korea's Policy Package for Enhancing its FTA Utilization and Implications for Korea's Policy*. ERIA Discussion Paper Series (ERIA-DP-2014–11).
3. Daniel, D., & Marc, D. F. (2007). *Deadlock in the Doha Round: The Long Decline of Trade Multilateralism*. Retrieved December 21, 2019, from https://www.worldtradelaw.net/articles/drachedoha.pdf.download.
4. European Commission. (2016). *EU Negotiating Texts in TTIP*. Retrieved December 21, 2019, from https://trade.ec.europa.eu/doclib/press/index.cfm?id=1230.
5. European Parliament. (2016). *TTIP: Access to Consolidated Texts and Confidential Documents*. Retrieved December 28, 2019, from https://www.europarl.europa.eu/RegData/etudes/BRIE/2016/580909/EPRS_BRI(2016)580909_EN.pdf#search=%27NPO+NGO+EU+TTIP%27.
6. European Commission. (2017). *Evaluation of the Implementation of the Free Trade Agreement between the EU and its Member States and the Republic of Korea*, p. 88. Retrieved December 21, 2019, from https://trade.ec.europa.eu/doclib/docs/2017/june/tradoc_155673.pdf.

7. European Commission. (2019).*EU Team in Korea for Government Consultations over Labour Commitments Under the Trade Agreement*. Retrieved December 21, 2019, from https://trade. ec.europa.eu/doclib/press/index.cfm?id=1973&title=EU-team-in-Korea-for-government-con sultations-over-labour-commitments-under-the-trade-agreement.
8. European Commission. (2006). Global Europe: Competing in the World. COM (2006) 567 final, September 4, 2006.
9. European Commission. (2007). *The Opinion of the European Court of Justice on the EU-Singapore Trade Agreement and the Division of Competences in Trade Policy*. Retrieved December 21, 2019, from https://trade.ec.europa.eu/doclib/docs/2017/september/tradoc_156 035.pdf.
10. European Commission. (2010). Europe 2020: A European Strategy for Smart, Sustainable and Inclusive Growth. COM (2010) 2020 final, March 3, 2010.
11. European Commission. (2010). Trade, Growth and World Affairs: Trade Policy as a Core Component of the EU's 2020 Strategy. COM (2010) 612 final, November 9, 2010.
12. European Commission. (2015). *Trade for All: Towards a More Responsible Trade and Investment Policy*. COM (2015) 497 final, September 15, 2015.
13. Ministry of Foreign Affairs of Japan. (2018). Agreement between the European union and Japan for an economic partnership. *Evaluation of the Implementation of the Free Trade Agreement between the EU and its Member States and the Republic of Korea*. Retrieved December 21, 2019, from https://www.mofa.go.jp/files/000382106.pdf.
14. New Zealand Foreign Affairs and Trade. (2016). *Trans-Pacific Partnership Agreement*. Retrieved December 21, 2019, from https://www.mfat.govt.nz/en/about-us/who-we-are/tre aties/trans-pacific-partnership-agreement-tpp/text-of-the-trans-pacific-partnership/.
15. Official Journal of the European Union. (2007). *Treaty of Lisbon Amending the Treaty on European Union and the Treaty Establishing the European Community*, 2007/C 306/01.
16. Official Journal of the European Union. (2011). *Council Decision of 16 September 2010 on the signing, on Behalf of the European Union, and Provisional Application of the Free Trade Agreement between the European Union and its Member States, of the One Part, and the Republic of Korea, of the Other Part* (2011/265/EU).
17. Official Journal of the European Union. (2012). *Consolidated Version of the Treaty on the Functioning of the European Union*, C 326. Retrieved October 26, 2012.
18. Pardo, R. P., Desmaele, L., & M. Ernst (2018). *EU-ROK Relations, Putting the Strategic Partnership to Work*. KF-VUB Korea Chair Report, October 2018. Retrieved December 21, 2019, from https://www.ies.be/files/EU-ROK_RELATIONS.pdf.
19. Shujiro, U. (2016). Mega-FTAs and the WTO: Competing or Complementary?*International Economic Journal, 30*(2).
20. Simon, J. E. (2005). *Competitive Liberalization: A Tournament Theory-Based Interpretation*. Retrieved December 24, 2019, from https://www3.nd.edu/~jbergstr/EvenettSept2005.pdf#sea rch=%27competitive+liberalization+Us%27.
21. Woolcock, S. (2007). *European Union Policy Towards Free Trade Agreements*. ECIPE Working Paper, No. 03/2007.

Chapter 3
The Korea–EU Trade Structure and Effects of Free Trade Agreement with Reductions in Tariffs and Non-tariff Measures

Chae-Deug Yi

Abstract This study examines the international trade structure between Korea and the EU in the 2010s and the economic effects of a Korea–EU FTA. First of all, to examine Korea's trade structure versus the EU's, this study used the Realized Comparative Advantage Index and Grubel-Lloyd Intra-Industry Trade index for Korea's 30 largest export items. Empirical results show that Korea's export items in general have comparative advantages against the EU and had low intra-industry trade structure in the 2010s. Then, this study used the standard CGE models to analyze economic effects of a bilateral Korea–EU FTA. The Korea–EU FTA with reduction of import tariffs and Non-Tariff Measures (NTMs) will increase Korea's GDP by 0.25% and improve the EU's GDP by 0.02%. Removing bilateral import tariffs and NTMs together lead to greater increases in GDP for both Korea and the EU than an FTA that removes only import tariffs or only NTMs. Korea and the EU can expect exports and imports of manufactured products to increase. However, Korea's exports to non-participating countries are expected to decline, and imports from non-participating countries such as Japan are also expected to decline across all sectors due to negative substitution effects.

Keywords Korea-EU FTA · Import tariff · Non-tariff measures · Trade policy

3.1 Introduction

In the 1960's, South Korea began a rapid transformation to become an industrialized country by focusing on its manufacturing industry and export-driven economic

The original version of this chapter was revised: Author names before the numbers preceding in-text bibliographical citations have been reinserted. The correction to this chapter is available at https://doi.org/10.1007/978-981-33-6145-4_7

C.-D. Yi (✉)
College of Economics and International Trade, Pusan National University, Busan, Republic of Korea
e-mail: givethanks@pusan.ac.kr

© Kobe University 2021, corrected publication 2021
M. Yoshii and C.-D. Yi (eds.), *An Economic Analysis of Korea–EU FTA and Japan–EU EPA*, Kobe University Monograph Series in Social Science Research, https://doi.org/10.1007/978-981-33-6145-4_3

growth. Beginning with its heavy chemical and light industries, Korea has emerged as one of the premier export-led nations, responding quickly to changes in technology and foreign investment, and periodically changing the focus of its industrial structure. Thus, exports and international trade are the major dynamic forces of economic growth in Korea and are highly significant for the country overall.

The EU is the world's largest economy and has been a leader on many issues globally. The EU has become an important trading partner for Korea, accounting for 30% of the country's current global economy. Korea has steadily expanded its free trade agreement (FTA) network since the Korea-Chile FTA was signed in 2004. As of 2019, Korea has FTAs with over 60 trading partners, including the world's top three economic blocs, the U.S., the EU, and ASEAN, as well as China and India. Since Korea–EU FTA negotiations concluded in September 2007 and the agreement became effective in July 2011, Korea and the EU have become active trading partners.

As FTAs, which remove import tariffs on trade among their members, have grown in number they have been the focus of many studies in recent years. FTAs are likely to have significant economic impacts on both FTA members and non-members,[1] and the impacts are greater if FTAs include contents other than trade liberalization. Thus, free trade and FTAs have been important to Korea's economic growth since the 1960s. As Lee [32] and Lee et al. [33] state, whether regional agreements are a facilitating intermediate step toward global free trade or to greater global trade liberalization is a hotly debated issue.[2]

Since there has been some disagreement regarding the effects of the Korea–EU FTA, it is worthwhile to examine its economic effects. Several studies related to Korea's trade and export expansion have been conducted. For example, Yi [41] examined the effects and implications of the Korea–EU FTA on Korea's trade. Previous studies on this topic have analyzed changes in tariffs and in the amount of trade, among other things, to assess the effect of the Korea–EU FTA.

Since the late 1980s, Computable General Equilibrium (CGE) models have been one of the main tools for evaluating FTAs, although there are some criticisms about using CGE models as noted by Ackerman and Gallagher [1]. According to Lee [32], CGE models capture extensive indirect effects, such as cross-industry linkages and trade linkages between countries and regions. They can also be used to evaluate the economic impacts of removing trade barriers on GDP, welfare, and trade flows for both member and non-member countries.

There have also been many studies of the economic effects of FTAs and trade liberalization globally, Brown and Stern [9] used a three-sector, 20-country CGE model that incorporates the behavior of multinational corporations and their foreign affiliates, and the international mobility of foreign direct investment capital, to assess the effects of the 33% reduction in tariffs and services barriers resulting from the Uruguay round of multilateral trade negotiations. They estimate that the combined reductions in tariffs and services barriers would increase global welfare by $193.2 billion. Ando and Urata [4] used a CGE model to analyze the impacts of East Asia

---

[1] See Ando and Urata [4].
[2] See, for example, [25, 29].

FTAs using a CGE model simulation, while Lee et al. [33] analyzed the APEC countries using CGE models.

Even though most studies predicted the trade effects of it before the Korea-EU FTA came into effect, a few studies use CGE models to analyze the effect of trade between Korea and the EU after the Korea–EU FTA was implemented. To analyze the effect of the Korea–EU FTA, Cooper et al. [11] examined its implications for the United States. Lakatos and Nilsson [30], and Forizs and Nilsson [17] examined the effects of the Korea–EU FTA using a comparative analysis of expected and observed outcomes. Ko [23] analyzed the Japan-EU FTA and Kim et al. [22] analyzed the economic impacts of Brexit using a CGE model.

However, Ecorys [16] reported that Non-Tariff Measures (NTMs) are more restrictive on US-EU trade and investment than tariffs. Therefore, this study uses both FTAs and NTMs as trade liberalization policy instruments. Raza et al. [38] criticized the fact that the estimated welfare gains in several studies of the Transatlantic Trade and Investment Partnership (TTIP) depend upon reductions of NTMs. As Nilsson [36] pointed out, the reduction of NTMs reduces trade costs through a separate provision of the TTIP agreement.[3] We note that successful harmonization of regulations, such as sanitary and phytosanitary (SPS) requirements, are an important achievement of any trade liberalization deal.

As Ando Urata [4] stated, it is increasingly important to examine the full impact of FTAs on economies by including a wide range of components. Therefore, this study attempts to estimate the comprehensive impacts of the Korea–EU FTA using a CGE approach. Although most previous simulation studies of the impacts of FTAs focus only on trade liberalization in product markets, our study attempts to take into account FTAs that involve both reductions of import tariffs and NTMs.

We analyze the Korea–EU FTA with its reductions of import tariffs and NTM issues in detail, to shed light on the full impact of the FTA. In particular, we assess the economic effects of the reduction of NTMs on GDP and trade using CGE models. To our knowledge, no study has yet analyzed the economic effects of the reduction in NTMs associated with the Korea–EU FTA. Thus, this study is unique in that we analyze the economic effects of not only removing import tariffs for manufactured products but also the impact on GDP and trade of reducing NTMs using CGE models, in the following ways.

First, we shed light on Korea's trade structure with the EU in the 2010s. We examined the Realized Comparative Advantage Index and Grubel-Lloyd Intra-Industry Trade Index for Korea's 30 largest export items versus the EU. Second, we analyze how removing mutual import tariffs through the Korea–EU FTA affects exports and imports using CGE models and simulation scenarios. We also examine how the Korea–EU FTA affects exports and imports, which ultimately leads to economic growth in Korea. Third, we use the CGE models and simulation scenarios to analyze how reducing NTMs between Korea and the EU affects exports and imports. Lastly, we analyze how simultaneously removing mutual import tariffs and reducing NTMs between Korea and EU affects exports and imports, based on the CGE models.

---

[3] According to [36], not all NTMs are non-tariff barriers (NTBs).

The remainder of this chapter is organized as follows. Part II provides a literature review. Part III shows Korea-EU trade structure. In Part IV, we use the CGE Model and data to simulate the impact of FTAs and NTMs. In Part V, we show the scenario of Korea-EU FTA. In Part VI, we analyze the results of the simulations. In Part VII, concludes and suggests areas for future research.

3.2 Literature Survey

There are two strands of research associated with the Korea–EU FTA: the trade structure approach, based on comparative advantage and intra-industry trade, and a CGE approach to examine the economic effects of the Korea–EU FTA on trade and GDP.

Korean researchers have studied trade patterns and intra-industry trade between Korea and the EU using a trade structure approach. In a study of Korean-EU trade patterns, Yi[43] analyzed Korea's trade trends with the EU using a Trade Specialization Index, Intra-Industry Trade and comparative advantage indexes, based on 3-digit Standard International Trade Classification (SITC) codes for specific products in the period 2007–2008. There are similarities between that study and this one in terms of evaluating Korea's trade structure quantitatively and with other practical measurers. Separately, Yi [44] analyzed product-based trade structure in 2003–2011 using industrial products according to SITC 3-digit codes and estimated the stability and flexibility of a comparative advantage index.

Since the Korea–EU FTA came into effect, several studies have focused on related trade and export expansion. Cooper et al. [11] examined the Korea-EU FTA and its implications for the United States. Norsten and Burlutska [37] analyzed interviews and trade statistics from Swedish manufacturing companies. Yi [44] verified the increase in Korea's export and import volumes on a product basis. Lakatos and Nilsson [30] examined anticipation, trade policy uncertainty, and the impact of the Korea-EU FTA.

Forizs and Nilsson [17] examined trade effects of the Korea-EU FTA using a comparative analysis of expected and observed outcomes. Using CGE models, Ko [23] analyzed the Japan-EU FTA, the Korea-USA FTA, and the Korea-China FTA, Kim et al. [22] analyzed Brexit and its economic and policy implications for Korea, and Song [39] examined the economic effects of the Japan-EU FTA on Korea. These studies use various methods of analysis such as changes in tariffs and the amount of trade, to evaluate the effect of the Korea–EU FTA. However, in most studies except for Kang and Kim [21], YI [44], it is rare to find an analysis of an FTA's effect by comparing intra-industrial trade and comparative advantage.

Dixon [13] and Hertel [19] provide overviews of the evolution in the use of CGE models in modeling trade policy. Nilsson [36] states that CGE models have been used to assess the economy-wide impact of trade liberalization and of trade policy for more than three decades. Krugman [26, 27] offered new trade theories in the form of scale economies and the varieties of imports. Melitz [35] introduced heterogeneous firms and argued that the more productive firms export, the least productive firms exit and that some of the less productive firms produce only for the domestic market. Costinot and Rodríguez-Clare [12] developed new trade theories following Melitz [35].

Attempts have been made to introduce Melitz-type structures in CGE models. Balistreri and Rutherford [8] introduced Melitz-type structures in CGE models and found significant productivity and variety effects. Zhai [45] implemented a simplified version of the Melitz model in a CGE framework and found that welfare gains from 50% tariff cuts worldwide roughly doubled compared to the regular Armington setting. Dixon et al. [14] derived Armington, Krugman, and Melitz models from a more general case and reproduced Melitz-type results. However, they did not find higher welfare effects in their specification compared to the Armington model. Arkolakis et al. [5], Akgul et al. [2], and Akgul [3] presented a new trade modeling framework taking firm heterogeneity into account and showed its importance for decomposing welfare changes. Nilsson [36] examined the economic modeling of FTAs.

Most of these studies were done after the Korea–EU FTA was implemented and focused on the removal of import tariffs with the EU using CGE models. As Nilsson [36] pointed out, however, the reduction of NTMs is also important as a trade liberalization policy instrument. So far, no study has analyzed economic effects on GDP and a trade of reduction in NTMs associated with the Korea–EU FTA. Therefore, unlike most previous studies, this chapter analyzes the economic effects on GDP and trade of the Korea–EU FTA including not only the removal of import tariffs but also reductions in NTMs using CGE models.

3.3 Trade Between Korea and the EU

3.3.1 Annual Trade Between Korea and the EU

In recent decades, the EU has become one of Korea's largest trading partners; since 2007, the EU has been Korea's second largest export destination and its third largest source of imports. Figure 3.1 shows Korea's annual exports to the EU, imports from the EU and Korea's trade balance versus the EU since 1988. While Korea recorded a trade surplus with the EU in the 1980s and a trade deficit in the beginning of the 1990s, during 1998–2002 Korea's imports decreased considerably due to the country's foreign exchange crisis in 1997. Thus, Korea recorded a trade surplus with the EU in 1998. In the second half of the 2000s, Korea's exports and trade balance increased considerably. In particular, Korea's trade surplus versus the EU jumped up from 5.5 billion US dollars in 2003 to 13.6 billion US dollars in 2004.

Korea's exports increased continuously until 2011, except in 2009 during the global financial crisis. However, Korea's exports decreased by 11.4% in 2012, and decreased further in 2013 due to the EU's government debt crisis, despite the introduction of the Korea–EU FTA in July 2011. Thus, Korea had a negative trade balance

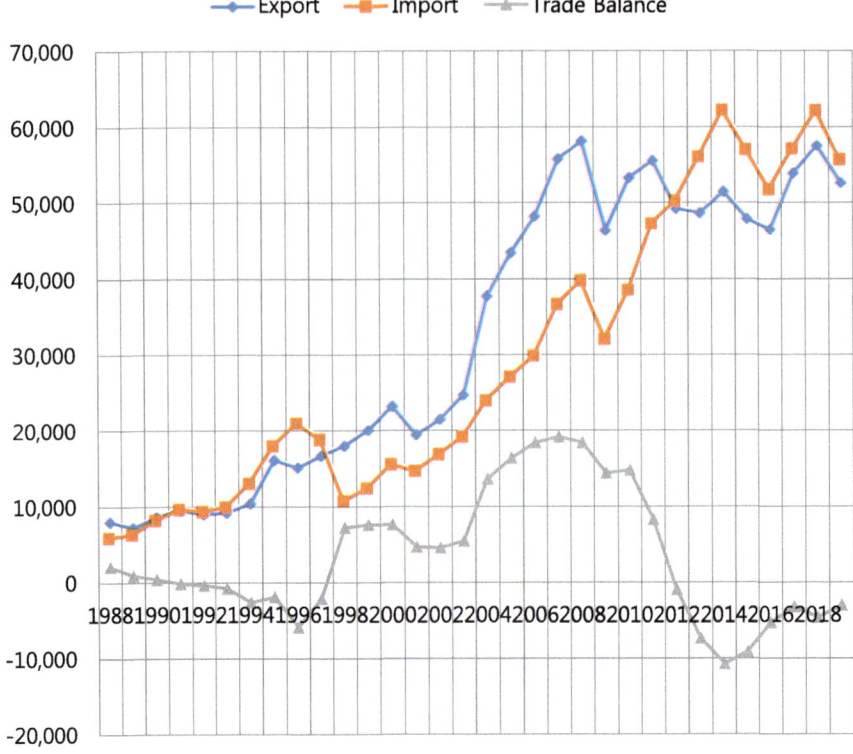

Fig. 3.1 Korea's trade versus EU (Year, Million US Dollar). *Source* Drawn using data from KITA, https://stat.kita.net

with the EU in 2012 and 2013. In 2012, Korea's exports were 49.4 billion USD and its imports were 50.4 billion USD, for a trade deficit with the EU of 1.0 billion USD. In 2013, Korea's exports declined to 48.4 billion USD but its imports increased by 11.6% to 56.2 billion USD, producing a large trade deficit of 7.3 billion USD.

As shown in Fig. 3.1, Korea's trade deficit versus the EU was largest in 2014, at 10.7 billion USD, when imports increased more than exports. Then, Korea's exports and imports both declined but the trade deficit became smaller. In 2015–2016, Korea's exports decreased, then increased in 2017 and 2018. In 2019, Korea's exports and imports decreased once again, so that exports reached 52.8 billion USD and imports were 55.8 billion USD. Korea's trade deficit versus the EU decreased from 4.6 to of 3.0 billion USD in 2019. Overall, Korea's trade deficit declined during 2014–2018.

3.3.2 Korea's 10 Largest Exports and Imports Versus the EU

Table 3.1 and Fig. 3.2 show Korea's exports to the EU by category, from largest to smallest, based on the 1-digit SITC commodity code. "Machinery and transport

Table 3.1 Ranking of Korea's Exports to the EU by category (2014–2019, million euro)

Code	Export category	2014	2015	2016	2017	2018	2019
		Value	Value	Value	Value	Value	Value
	Total	38,725,627	42,254,342	41,526,797	51,650,677	50,819,392	47,171,021
7	Machinery & transport equipment	23,748,405	26,417,471	25,195,424	31,491,411	30,998,979	28,667,596
6	Manufactured goods	4,807,575	5,311,239	5,754,958	6,401,441	7,185,696	6,506,243
8	Miscellaneous manufactured goods	3,290,956	3,262,807	2,996,549	2,710,701	2,717,763	2,802,383
5	Chemicals	3,871,260	4,724,596	5,198,077	8,540,550	7,588,091	6,867,280
3	Mineral fuels, lubricants	1,974,717	1,528,368	1,239,134	1,341,692	953,191	1,361,591
2	Crude material	696,165	575,311	551,727	594,378	684,597	608,848
9	Commodities not classified	152,392	179,386	300,592	241,304	384,996	7,264
0	Food & live animals	154,578	219,404	251,657	286,744	263,101	305,346
1	Beverage and tobacco	27,893	33,462	35,120	39,236	40,062	41,661
4	Animal and vegetable oils and fats	1,683	2,293	3,555	3,216	2,910	2,803

Source Calculated using data from KITA, https://stat.kita.net

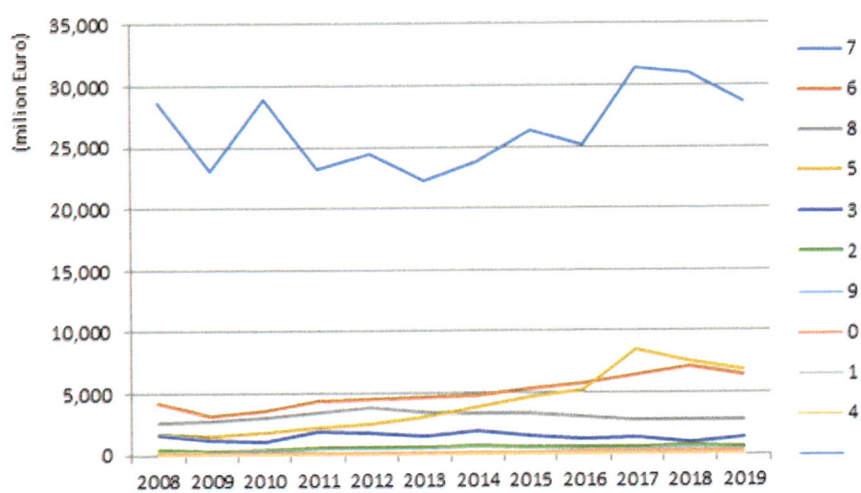

Fig. 3.2 Korea's export to the EU by 1-digit SITC code (Year, Million Euro). *Source* Drawn using the data from UNCTAD

equipment" (code 7) has been the largest export category since 2008. "Miscellaneous manufactured articles" (code 8) and "Manufactured goods classified chiefly by material" (code 6) have been the second or third largest export categories. The fourth largest category is "Mineral fuels, lubricants and related materials" (code 3) and the fifth largest is "Chemicals and related products" (code 5).

Table 3.2 and Fig. 3.3 show Korea's imports by category from the EU, from largest to smallest, using 1-digit SITC codes. "Machinery and transport equipment" (code 7) has been the largest import category since 2008. "Chemicals and related products" (code 5) has been second and "Miscellaneous manufactured articles" (code 8) has been the third largest import category. "Manufactured goods classified chiefly by material" (code 6) has been the fourth largest import category since 2008 and "Food and live animals" (code 0) has been the fifth largest since 2008.

"Machinery and transport equipment" (code 7) has been the largest category for both exports and imports since 2008 and we can see there has been a high degree of intra-industry trade in this category. However, in its trade with the EU, Korea has exported considerably more than it imported in this category since 2008, despite the implementation of the Korea–EU FTA in 2011.

Table 3.2 Ranking of Korea's Imports from the EU by category (2014–2019, million euro)

Code	Import commodity	2014	2015	2016	2017	2018	2019
		Value	Value	Value	Value	Value	Value
	Total	42,846,555	47,336,636	43,765,244	49,669,294	48,545,663	49,832,944
7	Machinery & transport equipment	21,568,212	24,307,115	22,007,000	24,954,252	23,811,833	23,890,715
5	Chemicals	6,023,008	6,498,587	7,005,105	7,314,086	7,741,125	8,542,772
6	Manufactured goods	3,863,624	3,883,703	3,651,907	3,730,476	3,782,507	4,253,769
8	Miscellaneous manufactured goods	4,446,868	5,216,684	5,540,597	6,429,799	6,303,294	7,793,393
0	Food & live animals	1,513,563	1,007,095	1,873,935	2,104,804	2,112,986	2,555,979
2	Crude material	1,016,183	1,684,054	813,426	907,357	960,240	1,101,444
3	Mineral fuels, lubricants	2,790,546	2,851,711	1,343,576	2,868,488	2,752,872	986,168
9	Commodities not classified	1,126,888	1,343,445	913,474	714,476	333,777	46,260
1	Beverage and tobacco	400,586	434,889	508,733	530,235	638,349	527,825
4	Animal and vegetable oils and fats	97,074	109,349	107,486	115,318	108,675	134,614

Source Calculated using data from KITA, https://stat.kita.net

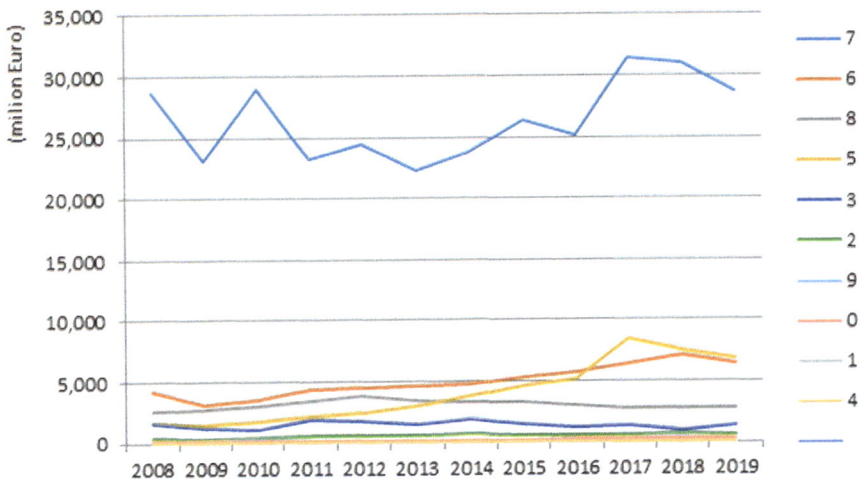

Fig. 3.3 Korea's import from the EU by 1-digit SITC code (Year, Million Euro). *Source* Drawn using the data from UNCTAD

With respect to "Miscellaneous manufactured articles" (code 8), while Korea exported slightly more than it imported during 2008–2011, in 2012 and 2013, after the Korea–EU FTA was implemented, Korea imported more of these products than it exported. The EU has had a comparative advantage in "Chemicals and related products" (code 5) since 2008. The EU exported goods in this category to Korea considerably more than it imported them from Korea even after the Korea–EU FTA was implemented in 2011.

3.3.3   Trade Structure Between Korea and the EU

As economic blocs and trade expand globally, it is important to study trade structure using the concept of comparative advantage and intra-industry trade indexes. Balassa and Bauwens [7] were based on earlier studies such as Krugman [25–28], Loertscher and Wolter 34, Lancaster [31], and Greenway and Milner [18]. In recent Korean studies of intra-industry trade, Yi [10, 41–44] analyzed Korea's comparative advantages and the structure of its intra-industry trade with the EU, China, and Japan.

Table 3.3 shows the Realized Comparative Advantage Index (RCA), standard Grubel-Lloyd Intra-Industry Trade Index, and trade disequilibrium Adjusted Grubel-Lloyd Intra-Industry Trade Index for Korea's 30 largest export items versus the EU by 2-digit SITC codes during 2017 and 2018. The numbers 17 and 18 appended to the index name represent the years 2017 and 2018.[4]

---

[4]See Yi [42].

Table 3.3 Korea's comparative advantage, intra-industry trade versus the EU (2017–2018)

Rank	Code	Category	RCA17	GLIIT17	AGLIIT17	RCA18	GLIIT18	AGLIIT18
1	87	Vehicles other than railway or tramway rolling-stock, and parts thereof	1.2819	0.90279	0.92748	1.296	0.90926	0.94568
2	84	Nuclear reactors, boilers, machinery,and mechanical appliances parts thereof	0.6458	0.75956	0.78033	0.726	0.80393	0.83613
3	85	Electrical machinery and equipment and parts thereof	1.5991	0.79487	0.81662	1.951	0.71259	0.74113
4	89	Ships, boats, and floating structures	81.5209	0.02555	0.02624	184.541	0.01164	0.0121
5	39	Plastics and articles thereof	2.4519	0.60155	0.61801	2.726	0.5676	0.59034
6	72	Iron and steel	4.7879	0.36104	0.37091	5.367	0.33507	0.34849
7	90	Optical, photographic, cinematographic, measuring, checking, precision, medical or surgical instruments and apparatus, parts, and accessories thereof	0.4783	0.624	0.64106	0.545	0.67066	0.69752
8	29	Organic chemicals	1.1761	0.94558	0.97145	1.141	0.97245	1.01139
9	40	Rubber and articles thereof	2.3078	0.62734	0.6445	2.96	0.53463	0.55605
10	30	Pharmaceutical products	0.3446	0.49248	0.50595	0.367	0.50756	0.52789
11	27	Mineral fuels. mineral oils, bituminous substances, mineral waxes	0.4656	0.61246	0.62922	0.262	0.38987	0.40549
12	73	Articles of iron or steel	1.106	0.97624	1.00295	1.309	0.904	0.94021
13	88	Aircraft, spacecraft, and parts thereof	2.9148	0.53141	0.54595	1.73	0.76871	0.7995
14	82	Tools, implements, cutlery, spoons, and forks, of base metal, and parts thereof	2.1551	0.65717	0.67515	2.279	0.64306	0.66881
15	38	Miscellaneous chemical products	0.3978	0.54776	0.56275	0.419	0.55886	0.58125
16	55	Man-made staple fibers	4.1886	0.4023	0.41331	5.354	0.33574	0.34918
17	54	Man-made filaments	5.3897	0.32732	0.33628	4.884	0.36219	0.3767
18	83	Miscellaneous articles of base metal	2.3037	0.62811	0.64529	2.547	0.59559	0.61945

(continued)

Table 3.3 (continued)

Rank	Code	Category	RCA17	GLIIT17	AGLIIT17	RCA18	GLIIT18	AGLIIT18
19	28	Inorganic chemicals, compounds of precious metals. rare-earth metals	0.217	0.34131	0.35064	0.273	0.40406	0.42024
20	76	Aluminum and articles thereof	0.3579	0.50671	0.52057	0.613	0.72438	0.75339
21	33	Essential oils and resinoids, perfumery, cosmetic, or toilet preparations	0.2166	0.34076	0.35008	0.294	0.42763	0.44476
22	60	Knitted or crocheted fabrics	6.5471	0.27749	0.28508	8.607	0.22299	0.23192
23	59	Impregnated, coated, covered, or laminated textile fabrics	3.1352	0.50345	0.51722	2.613	0.58487	0.6083
24	71	Pearls, precious or semi-precious stones, precious metals, coin	0.276	0.41479	0.42614	0.228	0.34812	0.36206
25	74	Copper and articles thereof	0.551	0.68631	0.70508	0.568	0.68914	0.71674
26	94	Furniture, bedding, mattresses, cushions, lamps &lighting fittings prefabricated buildings	0.4794	0.62499	0.64208	0.368	0.50826	0.52862
27	48	Paper and paperboard,articlesof paper pulp,of paper or of paperboard	0.4028	0.55277	0.56789	0.425	0.56471	0.58732
28	03	Fish, crustaceans, molluscs, other aquatic invertebrates	1.6604	0.77693	0.79818	1.138	0.97381	1.01281
29	32	Tanning or dyeing extracts, coloring matter, paints, putty,inks	0.3056	0.44925	0.46154	0.298	0.43234	0.44965
30	68	Articles of stone, plaster, cement, asbestos, mica, ceramicproducts	0.7722	0.84538	0.8685	1.06	0.99064	1.03032

Source Calculated using data from KITA, https://stat.kita.net

First, we note that the RCAs for "Vehicles other than railway or tramway rolling-stock, and parts" (code 87) were 1.27 in 2017 and 1.30 in 2018, so Korea has a comparative advantage in this category. Since both the standard Grubel-Lloyd IIT and AIIT Grubel-Lloyd IIT indexes are higher than 0.9, the level of IIT was very high between Korea and the EU for products in these categories, such as automobiles.

Second, since the RCAs of "Nuclear reactors, boilers, machinery and mechanical appliances parts" (code 84) in 2017 and 2018 were less than 1.0, Korea had a comparative disadvantage in these categories. The IIT indexes of this product were between 0.6 and 0.8, so the level of IIT is somewhat high between Korea and the EU.

Third, the RCAs of "Electrical machinery and equipment and parts" (code 85) were 1.60 in 2017 and 1.95 in 2018, which was somewhat higher than in 2015 and 2016. Thus, Korea had a comparative advantage in these categories relative to the EU market. Both the standard Grubel-Lloyd IIT and AIIT Grubel-Lloyd IIT indexes values were 0.7~0.8, so the level of IIT for these products appears to be quite high between Korea and the EU.

Fourth, the RCA of "Ships, boats, and floating structures" (code 89) was much higher than 1.0. Thus, Korea had a comparative advantage versus the EU despite an ongoing recession in the world shipbuilding industry. Since both the standard Grubel-Lloyd IIT and AIIT Grubel-Lloyd IIT Trade indexes were extremely low (0.01–0.02), the level of IIT appeared to be very low between Korea and the EU in this category during 2017 and 2018.

Fifth, "Plastics and articles thereof" (code 39), "Iron and steel" (code 72), and "Rubber and articles thereof" (code 40)" all have high comparative advantages in EU markets. However, since the levels of IIT in "Plastics and articles" (code 39) and "Iron and steel" (code 72) were from 0.3 to 0.4, the level of IIT between Korea and the EU was very low in 2017 and 2018.

In addition, the RCAs of "Aircraft, spacecraft and parts (code 88)", "Tools, implements, cutlery, spoons, and forks, of base metal and parts thereof" (code 82) were very high. Since the levels of IIT for this category was 0.5~0.6, the level of IIT was fairly high between Korea and the EU in 2017 and 2018.

RCAs for "Man-made filaments" (code 54), "Man-made staple fibers" (code 55), "Knitted or crocheted fabrics" (code 60), and "Impregnated, coated, covered, or laminated textile fabrics" (code 59) were much higher than 1.0; therefore, Korea had a comparative advantage in these categories in the EU during 2017 and 2018.

3.4   The CGE Model and Data

The CGE model used in this study is an extended version of the standard static GTAP model Hertel [20]. Economic agents consist of households, producers, and the government. The consumer is willing to maximize his utility according to a Cobb–Douglas utility function subject to budget constraints. The government purchases domestically produced and imported goods and services, based on a Cobb–Douglas aggregation function.

As in Ko [24], firms are expected to maximize their profits in both domestic and world commodity markets and factor markets under the constraint of production technology. The intermediate inputs and composites of capital and labor are used in fixed proportions to output. Capital and labor are combined through a Constant Elasticity of Substitution (CES) function to form the primary composite.

As in the Michigan CGE model, capital and labor are assumed to be perfectly mobile across sectors within each country. Within each region, commodity and factor prices equate demand and supply for all commodities and factors of production. World commodity prices are also expected to equate demand for imports and supply of exports by sector.

Following the Armington [6] Model, we assume that in international trade, domestic and imported goods are differentiated by region of origin and are modeled as imperfect substitutes. Products have different elasticities of substitution according to their region of origin. A CES specification is used to incorporate imperfect substitution of imported goods with respect to domestically produced goods. Thus, product differentiation between domestic goods and imports allows for intra-industry trade in each product category. The world market determines equilibrium prices such that all markets clear.

With respect to trade policies, we adopt the import tariff rates and NTMs that are applicable to bilateral trade between the various countries/regions. Revenues from import tariffs as well as rents from NTMs are redistributed to consumers in the tariff-levying country and are spent like other income.

Based on this standard CGE model, we use a multi-region, multi-sector approach to make a quantitative assessment of the economic effects of the Korea–EU FTA on Korea, Japan, the EU and The Rest of the World (ROW). The model includes four regions and 10 sectors. Since the Korea–EU FTA came into force in 2011, we use version 10 of the GTAP database that was released in 2019, with the base year of 2011. We analyze the effects of the Korea–EU FTA on Korea, the EU, Japan, and ROW.

The GTAP database divides the world into 141 regions, and each region has 65 sectors. Bilateral trade flows among the four countries/regions in our study are decomposed into 10 sectors. Trade with ROW is included to close the model. Table 3.4 shows the 141 regions aggregated into four regions. Table 3.5 shows 65 sectors combined into 10 sectors (Table 3.5).

Table 3.4 Regions used in the model

Country	Description
1 KOR	Korea
2 EU 28 Countries	EU 28 Countries
3 JPN	Japan
4 ROW	The rest of the world

Source Regional classification using GTAP DB Version 10 (2019)

Table 3.5 Sectors used in the model

No	Sector	Description
1	GrainCrops	Grains and Crops
2	MeatLvstk	Livestock and Meat Products
3	Extraction	Mining and Extraction
4	ProcFood	Processed Food
5	TextWapp	Textiles and Clothing
6	LightMnfc	Light Manufacturing
7	HeavyMnfc	Heavy Manufacturing
8	UtilCons	Utilities and Construction
9	TransComm	Transport and Communication
10	OthServices	Other Services

Source Classification of the products using GTAP DB Version 10 (2019)

3.5 Scenarios of Korea–EU Trade Liberalization Policies

We conduct three simulations in this study: a baseline scenario that includes some tariffs and NTMs, and two policy scenarios that eliminate bilateral tariffs with an FTA and/or reduce NTMs as a trade liberalization deal. As Ecorys [16] reported that NTMs impose more restrictions on U.S.-EU trade and investment than tariffs, we adopt FTAs and NTMs as policy instruments. Again, we acknowledge that the successful harmonization of regulations, such as SPS requirements, is an important component of trade liberalization deals.

3.5.1 Baseline Scenario

To assess the implications of a proposed free trade agreement, we first establish a baseline that shows the path of each economy in the absence of a Korea–EU FTA. In the baseline scenario, several key variables, including population and labor supply, are determined by exogenous assumptions.

The baseline scenario assumes that certain tariffs and NTMs, such as non-tariff barriers that existed before the Korea–EU FTA, are provisionally applied in July 2011. The EU-Korea FTA was formally adopted in December 2015, and the transitional period ended in 2016. Shocks for the baseline scenario include the implementation of the Korea–EU FTA.

The baseline scenario shows that economies are expected to have some tariffs and NTMs in the absence of an FTA or other trade liberalization deal, while the policy scenarios are used to assess the effects of the liberalization of trade by establishing an FTA that eliminates 100% of tariffs, or/and by reducing NTMs by 25%.

The difference between the baseline scenario and the policy scenarios shows the effects of the FTA and NTMs as the trade liberation policies on Korea, the EU, Japan, and ROW. Policy scenarios such as the Korea–EU FTA are considered by using updated and altered data from the baseline scenario.

3.5.2 Policy Scenarios

Three policy scenarios with respect to the Korea–EU FTA that include import tariffs and/or NTMs are conducted by eliminating tariffs and/or reducing NTMs or non-tariff barriers for manufactured goods, such as in trade liberalization agreements. Table 3.6 presents the three scenarios that include the elimination of bilateral tariffs with the Korea–EU FTA, or/and the reduction of NTMs via trade liberalization treaties.

In Scenario 1, Korea and the EU adopt a Korea–EU FTA to mutually eliminate tariffs on some manufactured imports by 100%. In Scenario 2, Korea and the EU mutually reduce NTMs only, by 25%, on all imports from the partner country. In Scenario 3, Korea and the EU adopt a Korea–EU FTA that mutually eliminates tariffs and reduces NTMs by 25%.

3.6 Simulation Results

Simulation results for the three scenarios are represented in terms of percentage changes in real GDP, export amount, import amount, and welfare level in each region. Since manufactured goods represent a large percentage of the trade between Korea and the EU, the simulation considers policy scenarios with reductions of tariffs and NTMs primarily in the Textiles and Clothing (TextWapp), Light Manufacturing (LightMnfc), and Heavy Manufacturing (HeavyMnfc) industries and product sectors.

Manufacturing liberalization is modeled according to the percentage reductions in import tariffs and NTMs for the EU and Korea as agreed upon in the Korea–EU FTA. Since the Korea–EU FTA came into force in 2011 and has been in existence for

Table 3.6 Three policy scenarios

Trade policies	Types	Level of trade liberalization
Scenario 1	Korea–EU FTA with Elimination of Tariffs	100% Tariff elimination
Scenario 2	Korea–EU FTA with a Reduction of NTMs only	Reduction of NTMs by 25%
Scenario 3	Korea–EU FTA with an Elimination of Tariffs and Reduction of NTMs	100% Tariff elimination and reduction of NTMs by 25%

Table 3.7 Impact on GDP of a Korea–EU FTA that eliminates tariffs (USD Million)

Nations	% change in GDP	GDP pre-FTA	GDP post FTA	Difference
EU_28	0.01	17,699,936	17,701,110	1,174
Korea	0.06	1,192,957	1,193,732	775
Japan	0	5,902,121	5,902,377	255.5
Rest of world	0	46,693,352	46,694,268	916

more than eight years,[5] we consider Korea and the EU to have reduced their bilateral import tariffs on manufactured products by 100%.

3.6.1 Scenario 1: Korea–EU FTA with Tariffs Eliminated

Table 3.7 reports the result of the simulation that models the impact on the GDPs of Korea, Japan, EU, and ROW of the Korea–EU FTA that eliminated 100% of the mutual import tariffs on manufactured goods for sectors such as TextWapp, LightMnfc, and HeavyMnfc.

Table 3.7 presents the percentage changes in GDP for Korea, the EU, Japan, and ROW resulting from the Korea–EU FTA. In the absence of positive externalities, the Korea–EU FTA would have had very little impact on GDP for Korea or the EU, primarily because the share of the EU's trade with Korea represented less than 5% of total EU trade in 2019. Thus, with a Korea–EU FTA that eliminates import tariffs for three industrial sectors, we would expect Korea's GDP to rise by 0.06%, and would expect the EU's GDP to increase by 0.01%. Thus, a Korea–EU FTA that eliminates import tariffs in these three sectors would have a positive effect on GDP for both entities. There would also be a small impact on non-participating countries such as Japan, and on the rest of world.

As shown in Tables 3.7, an FTA that eliminates import tariffs is more preferable to a small, open economy such as Korea compared to a large economy such as the EU. The GDPs of non-participating countries such as Japan and ROW also benefit, but not significantly.

3.6.1.1 Exports from Korea

Table 3.8 shows the impact (in percentage terms) of a Korea–EU FTA that eliminates 100% of import tariffs for goods from the TextWapp, LightMnfc, and HeavyMnfc industries on Korea's exports to the EU. The FTA would have a limited impact on Korea's exports of products other than the TextWapp, LightMnfc, and HeavyMnfc industries to the EU, as well as to Japan and ROW.

---

[5]Korea and the EU agreed to abolish import tariffs on manufactured goods over the seven years since the Korea-EU FTA came into force in July 2011.

The proposed Korea–EU FTA would have a large impact on Korean exports to the EU in three manufacturing sectors. The model shows exports from Korea to the EU would increase by 86.06% in the TextWapp sector, by 38.62% in the LightMnfc sector, and by 34.18% in the HeavyMnfc sector. However, Korean exports to non-participating countries from these three sectors are expected to decline by 3–5%. In this scenario, Korea's exports to Japan decrease by 4.13% in the TextWapp sector, by 4.82% in the LightMnfc sector, and by 3.45% in the HeavyMnfc sector. Korea's exports to ROW also decrease by 3.47% in TextWapp, by 3.97% in LightMnfc, and by 3.10% in HeavyMnfc. Korea's exports to the EU, Japan, and ROW in other sectors would decline due to the substitution effects of import tariff elimination in the TextWapp, LightMnfc, and HeavyMnfc sectors.

3.6.1.2 Exports from the EU

Table 3.9 shows the impact of the Korea–EU FTA with 100% mutual import tariff reductions on changes in exports from the EU to other countries. Exports from the EU to Korea are expected to increase by 3.47% in the TextWapp sector, by 12.98% in the LightMnfc sector, by 3.69% in the HeavyMnfc sector. However, exports from the EU to Japan are expected to decrease in all sectors except for Extraction, TextWapp and HeavyMnfc, which are expected to increase by 0.78, 0.04 and 0.11%, respectively. Exports from the EU to ROW are expected to increase across all sectors.

3.6.1.3 Exports from Japan

Table 3.10 shows the impact of the Korea–EU FTA that eliminates import tariffs between the two parties on exports from Japan. Exports from Japan to the EU are expected to rise by 1.37% in the TextWapp sector, by 1.36% in the LightMnfc sector, and by 1.48% in the HeavyMnfc sector. Exports from Japan to Korea and ROW are

Table 3.8 Impact on Korea's exports resulting from a Korea–EU FTA (in %)

Korea's exports	EU_28	Japan	Rest of world
GrainsCrops	−1.03	−1.19	−0.86
MeatLvstk	−3.67	−3.72	−3.18
Extraction	−3.51	−2.54	−3.48
ProcFood	−1.86	−2.41	−1.54
TextWapp	86.06	−4.13	−3.47
LightMnfc	38.62	−4.82	−3.97
HeavyMnfc	34.18	−3.45	−3.1
Util_Cons	−3.32	−3.91	−3.09
TransComm	−3.21	−3.87	−2.97
OthServices	−3.75	−4.29	−3.52

Table 3.9 Impact on EU's
exports resulting from a
Korea–EU FTA (in %)

EU's exports	Korea	Japan	Rest of world
GrainsCrops	0.24	−0.25	0.23
MeatLvstk	1.62	−0.22	0.46
Extraction	−0.03	0.78	0.09
ProcFood	0.97	−0.55	0.34
TextWapp	3.47	0.04	0.68
LightMnfc	12.98	−0.45	0.54
HeavyMnfc	3.69	0.11	0.46
Util_Cons	1.47	−0.49	0.36
TransComm	1.58	−0.63	0.30
OthServices	2.04	−0.48	0.32

Table 3.10 Impact on Japan's exports resulting from a Korea–EU FTA (in %)

Japan's exports	EU_28	Korea	Rest of world
GrainsCrops	1.36	1.55	1.47
MeatLvstk	2.09	3.64	2.5
Extraction	1.94	1.57	1.67
ProcFood	1.18	2.13	1.5
TextWapp	1.37	4.18	2.15
LightMnfc	1.36	2.65	2.39
HeavyMnfc	1.48	2.69	2.1
Util_Cons	1.49	2.85	1.74
TransComm	1.37	2.91	1.62
OthServices	1.48	3.47	1.73

expected to increase in all sectors by 1% to 5%, with changes that are often larger
on a percentage basis than the changes in Japan's exports to the EU.

3.6.1.4   World Imports

Table 3.11 summarizes changes in imports to the EU, Korea, Japan and ROW based
on a Korea–EU FTA that removes 100% of imports tariffs between those two entities. Imports by Korea from all countries are expected to increase by 2.18% in the
TextWapp sector, by 3.80% in the LightMnfc sector, and by 1.35% in the HeavyMnfc
sector. Imports into Korea in all other sectors except for Extraction are also expected
to rise. This increase is likely due to the increase in Korea's GDP resulting from

Table 3.11 Impact on World's imports of Korea–EU FTA (in %)

Import sector	EU_28	Korea	Japan	Rest of world
GrainsCrops	−0.03	0	−0.48	0.02
MeatLvstk	−0.07	1.21	−0.66	0.06
Extraction	0.01	−0.2	0.61	−0.08
ProcFood	−0.06	0.71	−0.9	0.07
TextWapp	0	2.18	−0.66	0.01
LightMnfc	0.17	3.8	−1.1	0.08
HeavyMnfc	0.06	1.35	−0.67	0.02
Util_Cons	−0.09	1.52	−1.43	0.07
TransComm	−0.08	1.43	−1.01	0.11
OthServices	−0.09	1.81	−0.87	0.09

the Korea–EU FTA with 100% tariff reductions for the TextWapp, LightMnfc, and HeavyMnfc sectors.

With a Korea–EU FTA, EU imports for the TextWapp sector are expected to remain largely unchanged, while imports for the LightMnfc and HeavyMnfc sectors are expected to increase by 0.17% and 0.06%, respectively. However, imports by the EU for all other sectors is expected to decrease, except for the Extraction sector. Imports by Japan in the TextWapp sector are expected to decrease by 0.66%, LightMnfc imports are expected to decrease by 1.10%, and HeavyMnfc imports are expected to decrease by 0.67%. Imports by Japan in all other sectors are expected to decrease except in the Extraction sector, due to the substitution effects of import tariff elimination.

Thus, with a Korea–EU FTA, the EU and Korea are expected to increase imports in the TextWapp, LightMnfc, and HeavyMnfc industries, but non-participating Japan is expected to decrease imports in those sectors as well as all other industries except Extraction. ROW is expected to increase imports from the TextWapp, LightMnfc, and HeavyMnfc sectors.

In this scenario, where the Korea–EU FTA eliminates import tariffs in three manufacturing sectors, trade between Korea and the EU increases appreciably in those three sectors, and in other sectors. In perfectly competitive trade models such as the Heckscher-Ohlin Model, one expects countries as a whole to gain from trade. However, Stolper and Samuelson [40] argued the owners of a scarce factor of production lose. Gains from additional sources of trade will have increasing returns to scale, competition, and product variety based on the new trade model in our CGE modeling.

Another important result that emerges from this scenario is that trade with the ROW also changes somewhat significantly. Bilateral trade between Korea and the EU expands in the three manufactured product sectors, but trade with the ROW contracts. That is, trade liberalization permits Korea and the EU to expand their exports, which allows these sectors to be more competitive with a larger number of competing entities abroad. According to new trade models such as in Krugman [27],

Korea and the EU as a whole gain from lower costs due to increasing returns to scale from greater competition, and as trade partners they have increased their utility due to greater product variety. All of these effects make it more likely that countries will gain from liberalization that accompanies a reduction of import tariffs.

3.6.2 Scenario 2: Korea–EU FTA with a Reduction of NTMs

3.6.2.1 World GDP

Table 3.12 shows the percentage changes in GDP for Korea, Japan, EU, and ROW from a Korea–EU FTA that includes only a 25% reduction in mutual NTMs for the TextWapp, LightMnfc, and HeavyMnfc sectors.

In Scenario 2, Korea's GDP is expected to rise by 0.20% and the EU's GDP is expected to rise by 0.02%. Interestingly, liberalizing Korea–EU trade by reducing NTMs by 25% in the three sectors leads to increases in GDP for both Korea and the EU that are larger than with an FTA that removes import tariffs. Furthermore, Scenario 2, which reduces NTMs by 25%, is more favorable than Scenario 1, which eliminates import tariffs, in terms of the increase in GDP for both Korea and the EU. The impact on GDP for non-participating countries such as Japan and ROW's is close to zero.

Table 3.12 Impact on GDP of 25% reduction in Korea and EU's NTMs (USD Million)

Nations	% Change in GDP	Pre-FTA	Post FTA	Difference
EU_28	0.02	17,699,936	17,704,020	4,084
Korea	0.20	1,192,957	1,195,369	2,412
Japan	0	5,902,121	5,902,088	−33
Rest of World	0	46,693,352	46,692,652	−700

3.6.2.2 Korea, the EU, and Japan Export

Tables 3.13, 3.14, and 3.15 show the impact of Korea's and the EU's 25% mutual reduction in NTMs in the TextWapp, LightMnfc, and HeavyMnfc sectors in terms of changes in exports from Korea, the EU and Japan. As shown in Table 3.13, exports from Korea to the EU are expected to rise in TextWapp, LightMnfc, and HeavyMnfc by 24.55, 20.35, and 23.43%, respectively. However, Korean exports to the EU are expected to decline by 1% to 3% in all other sectors, and to decline in every sector for all non-participating countries.

In scenario 1, Korea's export to Japan decrease in TextWapp by 2.06%, LightMnfc by 2.42%, and HeavyMnfc by 1.72%, respectively. Korea's exports to ROW in

Table 3.13 Effects on	Korea's export	EU_28	Japan	Rest of world
Korea's exports of Korea–EU's 25% reduction of NTMs (% change)	GrainsCrops	−0.76	−0.72	−0.8
	MeatLstk	−2.38	−2.41	−2.48
	Extraction	−2.78	−2.52	−2.71
	ProcFood	−1.09	−1.18	−1.18
	TextWapp	24.55	−2.06	−2.01
	LightMnfc	20.35	−2.42	−2.41
	HeavyMnfc	23.43	−1.72	−1.72
	Util_Cons	−2.04	−1.97	−2.12
	TransComm	−2.15	−2.2	−2.2
	OthServices	−2.6	−2.68	−2.67

TextWapp, Light Mnfc, and HeavyMnfc decline by 2.01%, 2.41%, and 1.72%, respectively. Korea's exports in the other sectors also decline as shown in Table 3.12.

As shown in Table 3.14, with a 25% reduction in NTMs between Korea and the EU for the manufacturing three sectors, exports from the EU to Korea are expected to increase in those sectors. However, exports from the EU to Japan are expected to decrease in all sectors except for an increase of 0.11% in the UtilCons sector. EU exports to all other non-participating countries are expected to decrease in all sectors except for an increase in UtilCons of 0.02%.

As shown in Table 3.15, with the 25% reduction of NTMs in the three manufacturing sectors, Japan's exports to the EU are expected to rise slightly in those sectors. Exports from Japan to Korea are expected to decrease by 0.78%, 2.08%, and 1.29% in TextWapp, LightMnfc, and HeavyMnfc, respectively.

Table 3.14 Effects on EU	EU's export	Korea	Japan	Rest of world
exports of Korea–EU reductions of NTMs (% change)	GrainsCrops	−0.01	−0.1	−0.09
	MeatLstk	0.64	−0.18	−0.17
	Extraction	−0.24	−0.1	−0.1
	ProcFood	0.5	−0.1	−0.1
	TextWapp	21.6	−0.12	−0.09
	LightMnfc	17.25	−0.04	0.02
	HeavyMnfc	19.99	−0.01	−0.01
	Util_Cons	0.98	0.11	−0.04
	TransComm	1.01	−0.06	−0.07
	OthServices	1.28	−0.1	−0.08

Table 3.15 Effects on Japan's exports of Korea–EU FTA with a reduction of NTMs (% change)

Japan's exports	EU_28	Korea	Rest of world
GrainsCrops	0.09	0.12	0.03
MeatLvstk	0.23	0.88	0.07
Extraction	−0.04	−0.23	−0.09
ProcFood	0.14	0.65	0.05
TextWapp	0.01	−0.78	0.09
LightMnfc	−0.2	−2.08	0.17
HeavyMnfc	−0.13	−1.29	0.12
Util_Cons	0.2	1.14	0.12
TransComm	0.14	1.16	0.08
OthServices	0.17	1.46	0.1

3.6.2.3 World Imports

Table 3.16 shows the impact on imports for Korea, Japan, the EU, and ROW, given trade liberalization between Korea and the EU involving a 25% reduction of mutual NTMs for the TextWapp, LightMnfc, and HeavyMnfc sectors.

World imports from in both Korea and the EU are expected to increase in the TextWapp, LightMnfc, and HeavyMnfc sectors. The percentage changes in Korea are greater than in the EU under this scenario. Imports in all other sectors except extraction are expected to increase in both Korea and the EU. However, non-participating Japan and ROW are expected to decrease imports in all sectors due to Korea's and the EU's reduction of NTMs in the TextWapp, LightMnfc, and HeavyMnfc sectors.

We derive an important result from this scenario of reduced NTMs, namely that trade with bilateral trade partners increases significantly in sectors where NTMs are reduced, but trade with Japan and ROW declines significantly in almost all sectors due to substitution effects between participating and non-participating countries. Liberalization of NTMs reduces or eliminates quota rents, customs formality, trade costs, and other NTMs and could lead to an increase in trade efficiency between Korea and the EU.

3.6.3 Scenario 3: Korea–EU FTA with Reductions of Tariffs and NTMs

3.6.3.1 World GDP

Table 3.17 shows the impact on the EU, Korea, Japan, and ROW of trade liberalization between Korea and the EU that includes both 100% import tariff reductions and 25% reductions in NTMs for the TextWapp, LightMnfc, and HeavyMnfc sectors.

In Scenario 3, Korea's GDP is expected to rise by 0.25% while the EU's GDP rises by 0.02%. Thus, this trade policy would have positive effects on GDP for both

Table 3.16 Effects of Korea and EU's reduction of NTMs on world's imports

Import sectors	EU_28	Korea	Japan	Rest of world
GrainsCrops	0.01	0.06	−0.02	−0.02
MeatLvstk	0.03	0.8	−0.02	−0.03
Extraction	−0.01	−0.16	−0.01	−0.02
ProcFood	0.02	0.6	−0.05	−0.02
TextWapp	0.08	1.25	−0.03	−0.04
LightMnfc	0.16	3.84	−0.1	−0.08
HeavyMnfc	0.09	1.53	−0.1	−0.05
Util_Cons	0.01	1.04	−0.3	−0.08
TransComm	0.03	1.09	−0.08	−0.04
OthServices	0.03	1.38	−0.08	−0.05

Table 3.17 Impact on GDP of Korea–EU reductions of tariffs and NTMs (USD Million)

Nations	% changes of GDP	Pre	Post	Changes
EU_28	0.02	17,699,936	17,702,970	3,034
Korea	0.25	1,192,957	1,195,930	2,973
Japan	0	5,902,121	5,902,075	−46
Rest of World	0	46,693,352	46,692,840	−512

of Korea and the EU. Moreover, Korea's GDP increases more in Scenario 3 than in Scenario 1 and Scenario 2. Scenario 3 increases the EU's GDP more than Scenario 1 and slightly more than in Scenario 2 but the difference is not significant. GDP in non-participating Japan and for ROW declines slightly but the change is not significantly different from zero.

3.6.3.2 Korea, the EU, and Japan Export

Tables 3.18, 3.19, and 3.20 show the impact on exports of an agreement between Korea and the EU to remove import tariffs and reduce NTMs by 25% in the TextWapp, LightMnfc, and HeavyMnfc sectors. As shown in Table 3.18, exports from Korea to the EU are expected to rise by 36.74% in TextWapp, and by 30.77% in LightMnfc, but are expected to fall in HeavyMnfc by 0.89%. Exports from Korea to all other non-participating countries are expected to decline 1–4% across all sectors.

As shown in Table 3.19, exports from the EU to Korea are expected to rise by 29.84% in TextWapp, and by 22.94% in LightMnfc, but are expected to fall in HeavyMnfc by 26.47%. Exports from the EU to Japan are expected to decrease across all sectors by 0.03–0.27%, while exports from the EU to ROW are expected to decrease across all sectors by 0.09–0.24%.

Table 3.18 Korea–EU's removal of tariffs and reduction of NTMs on Korea's exports

Korea's exports	EU_28	Japan	Rest of world
GrainsCrops	−0.6	−0.62	−0.67
MeatLvstk	−1.84	−1.98	−2.01
Extraction	−2.07	−1.98	−2.11
ProcFood	−0.81	−0.96	−0.93
TextWapp	36.74	−1.26	−1.22
LightMnfc	30.77	−1.63	−1.58
HeavyMnfc	−0.89	−1.06	−1.00
Util_Cons	−1.49	−1.54	−1.62
TransComm	−1.68	−1.79	−1.77
OthServices	−2.1	−2.24	−2.19

Table 3.19 Impact on EU exports of Korea–EU tariff removal and reduction of NTMs

EU's export	Korea	Japan	Rest of world
GrainsCrops	−0.07	−0.16	−0.14
MeatLvstk	0.64	−0.27	−0.24
Extraction	−0.86	−0.2	−0.19
ProcFood	0.36	−0.17	−0.14
TextWapp	29.84	−0.22	−0.18
LightMnfc	22.94	−0.17	−0.09
HeavyMnfc	26.47	−0.21	−0.16
Util_Cons	0.73	−0.03	−0.11
TransComm	0.75	−0.14	−0.11
OthServices	1.02	−0.17	−0.12

Table 3.20 Effects on Japan's exports of Korea–EU tariff removal and reduction of NTMs

Japan's exports	EU_28	Korea	Rest of world
GrainsCrops	0.17	0.15	0.08
MeatLvstk	0.37	1.02	0.15
Extraction	0.1	−0.71	−0.04
ProcFood	0.22	0.6	0.1
TextWapp	0.06	−1.04	0.14
LightMnfc	−0.23	−3.32	0.22
HeavyMnfc	0.3	−2.47	0.18
Util_Cons	0.3	1.01	0.17
TransComm	0.22	1	0.14
OthServices	0.25	1.3	0.15

Table 3.21 Effects of Korea–EU's removal of tariffs and reduction of NTMs on world import

Import sector	EU_28	Korea	Japan	Rest of world
GrainsCrops	0.01	0.06	−0.03	−0.02
MeatLstk	0.03	0.86	−0.04	−0.03
Extraction	0.08	−0.69	−0.02	−0.01
ProcFood	0.02	0.5	−0.07	−0.03
TextWapp	0.1	1.72	−0.04	−0.04
LightMnfc	0.23	4.72	−0.12	−0.06
HeavyMnfc	0.04	1.35	−0.12	−0.04
Util_Cons	0.04	0.83	−0.29	−0.08
TransComm	0.04	0.88	−0.1	−0.04
OthServices	0.04	1.15	−0.11	−0.06

As shown in Table 3.20, in Scenario 3, exports from Japan to the EU are expected to rise in TextWapp and in HeavyMnfc, but are expected to decrease in LightMnfc. Exports from Japan to Korea are expected to decrease by 1.04% in TextWapp, by 3.32% in LightMnfc, and by 12.47% in HeavyMnfc due to trade liberalization between Korea and the EU.

3.6.3.3 World Imports

Table 3.21 shows the impact of Scenario 3's trade liberalization between Korea and the EU on imports for Korea, Japan, the EU, and ROW. Both the EU and Korea are expected to increase imports in TextWapp, LightMnfc, and HeavyMnfc, with increases in Korea much larger than in the EU on a percentage basis. However, non-participating countries such as Japan and ROW are expected to decrease their imports in TextWapp, LightMnfc, and HeavyMnfc and in all other sectors by 0.01–0.29%.

Due to the reductions of import tariffs and NTMs between Korea and the EU, increased competition raises total factor productivity. Reductions in export prices of goods produced in Korea and the EU lead to export expansion for the bilateral partners in the three manufacturing sectors. However, the effects on the welfare of these countries depends on a mixture of the substitution effects between products, terms-of-trade effects, and standard efficiency gains from conventional trade theory. We expect on average that Korea and the EU will gain from bilateral liberalization, as resources are reallocated to those sectors in the respective country where there is a comparative advantage. In addition, Korea and the EU will take advantage of scale economies and preferences for variety proposed by new trade theories. In the absence of terms-of-trade effects, trade liberalization can raise the national welfare levels of Korea and the EU.

3.7   Conclusion

This study examines the international trade structure between Korea and the EU in the 2010s and the economic effects on Korea, the EU, Japan, and ROW of a bilateral Korea–EU FTA. First of all, to examine Korea's trade structure versus the EU's, we used the Realized Comparative Advantage Index and Grubel-Lloyd Intra-Industry Trade index for Korea's 30 largest export items versus the EU. Empirical tests show that Korea's main export items in general have comparative advantages against the EU and low intra-industry trade structure in the 2010s.

Then, this study used a 4-region, 10-sector CGE model to examine the economic effects of a bilateral Korea–EU FTA. The scenarios incorporated trade liberalization for three manufacturing sectors, namely reductions in import tariffs and/or reductions in NTMs such as customs or trade costs. The main results are summarized as follows.

First, a Korea–EU FTA that removes import tariffs has a positive impact on GDP for both countries participating in the bilateral agreement, in this case Korea and the EU, with Korea's GDP increasing more than the EU's GDP on a percentage basis. However, the Korea–EU FTA does not lead to a significant increase in GDP for non-participating countries such as Japan and ROW.

Second, a Korea–EU FTA with a 25% reduction of NTMs is more beneficial than an agreement that removes import tariffs in terms of the increases in GDP for both FTA participants. The GDPs for non-participating countries such as Japan and ROW's declined slightly in this scenario but the changes are not significant.

Third, a Korea–EU FTA that removes tariffs and reduces NTMs increased Korea's GDP by 0.25% and improved EU's GDP by 0.02%. Thus, this trade policy have positive effects on GDPs for both participants. As in the second scenario, the GDPs for non-participating Japan and ROW decline slightly but the changes are close to zero.

Fourth, in all three scenarios Korea and the EU can expect exports and imports of manufactured products to increase. However, Korea's exports to non-participating countries are expected to decline, and imports of non-participating countries (e.g., Japan and ROW) are expected to decline across all sectors due to negative substitution effects.

Thus, a Korea–EU FTA is expected to have a positive impact on the two participating economies. Removing bilateral trade barriers and NTMs together lead to greater increases in GDP for both Korea and the EU than an FTA that only removes import tariffs, and also increases bilateral trade between Korea and the EU. The Korea–EU FTA would also lead to more competition and improve production efficiency. Furthermore, the Korea–EU FTA can contribute not only to bilateral trade between Korea and the EU but also to global income and free trade.

One limitation of our CGE model is that it is based on a static approach, meaning that all of the trade liberalization occurs simultaneously. In the real world, these effects occur over time. Our results would also be more accurate with respect to the economic benefits if we considered the elasticities of supply and demand, and foreign direct investment. However, we will leave this for a future study.

Acknowledgements This work was supported under the framework of international cooperation program managed by the National Research Foundation of Korea (2018K2A9A2A08000161, FY2018).

References

1. Ackerman, F., & Gallagher, K. P. (2014). The shrinking gains from global trade liberalization in computable general equilibrium models: A critical assessment. *International Journal of Political Economy, 37*(1), 50–77.
2. Akgul, Z. (2017). One Model To Rule Them All? The Importance of Firm Heterogeneity in CGE Modeling of the Gains from Trade, USITC Economics Working Paper 3-B.
3. Akgul, Z., Villoria, N. B., & Hertel, T. W. (2016). GTAP-HET: Introducing firm heterogeneity into the GTAP Model. *Journal of Global Economic Analysis, 1*, 111–180.
4. Ando, M., & Urata, S. (2007). The impacts of East Asia FTA: A CGE model simulation Study. *Journal of International Economic Studies, 11*(2), 3–57.
5. Arkolakis, C., Costinot, A., & Rodríguez-Clare, A. (2012). New trade models, same old gains? *American Economic Review, 102*(1), 94–130.
6. Armington, P. S. (1969). A theory of demand for products distinguished by place of production. *IMF Staff Papers, 16*(1), 159–178.
7. Balassa, B., & Bauswens, L. (1988). *Changing trade patterns in manufactured good.* Amsterdam: North Holland.
8. Balistreri,E. J., & Rutherford, T. F. (2013). Computing general equilibrium theories of monopolistic competition and heterogeneous firms, Chapter 23. In. *Handbook of Computable General Equilibrium Modelling* (Vol. 1, pp. 1513–1570). Elsevier.
9. Brown, D. K., & Stern, R. M. (2001). Measurement and modeling of the economic effects of trade and investment barriers in services. *Review of International Economics, 9*(2), 262–286.
10. Chang, M. S. (2017). An analysis on trade competitiveness of Korean automobile industry. *Koreanische Zeitschrift Fuer Wirtschaftswissenschaften, 35*(4), 169–193.
11. Cooper, W. H., Jurenas, R., Platzer, M. D., & Manyin, M. E. (2011). *The EU-South Korea free trade agreement and its implications for the United States*, CRS report for congress 7–5700.
12. Costinot, A., & Rodríguez-Clare, A. (2014). Trade theory with numbers: quantifying the consequences of globalization. *Handbook of international economics.4*, 197–261.
13. Dixon, P. (2006). *Evidence-based trade policy decision making in Australia and the development of computable general equilibrium modelling.* Centre of Policy Studies: Monash University, Australia.
14. Dixon, P., Jerie, M., & Rimmer, M. (2016). Modern trade theory for CGE modelling: The Armington, Krugman and Melitz models. *Journal of Global Economic Analysis, 1*(1), 1–110.
15. Dixon, P., Jerie, M., & Rimmer, M. (2018). *Trade theory in computable general equilibrium models, Armington.* Springer Nature Singapore Pte Ltd: Krugman and Melitz.
16. Ecorys. (2009). Non-tariff measures in EU-US trade and investment—an economic analysis, final report (reference: OJ 2007/S 180–219493) for the European Commission, DG trade.
17. Forizs, V., & Nilsson, L. (2017). Trade effects of the EU-Korea free trade agreement: A comparative analysis of expected and observed outcomes. *Estey Journal of International Law and Trade Policy, 18*(1), 14–30.
18. Greenaway,D., & Milner C. (1984). A cross section analysis of intra-industry trade in the U.K.*European Economic Review, 25*(3), 319–344.
19. Hertel, T. W. (2013). Global applied general equilibrium analysis using the global trade analysis project framework. In P. B. Dixon & D. W. Jorgenson (Eds.), *Handbook of computable general equilibrium modeling, 1* (pp. 815–876). Amsterdam: Elsevier.

20. Hertel, T. W. (1997). *Global trade Analysis: Modeling and Applications*, Cambridge University Press.
21. Kang, Y., & Kim, J. (2013). Trade and investment Between Korea and EU after the Korea-Japan-EU FTA and its prospect. *World Economy, 3*(44), 1–9.
22. Kim, H.-C., Kim, Y.-G., Han, M. S., Kim, J.-D., Cho, M.-H., & Lim, Y.-J. (2016). *Economic impacts of brexit and its policy implications to Korea* (pp. 16–17). KIEP: Public Analysis.
23. Ko, J. (2014). Economic assessment of Korea-Japan-EU FTA using a CGE model with FDI. *Journal of European Union Studies, 36*, 37–71.
24. Ko, J. (2019). RCEP and its impact on the global economy: A CGE approach.
25. Krueger, A. O. (1999). Are preferential trading arrangements trade-liberalizing or protectionist? *Journal of Economic Perspectives, 13*(4), 105–124.
26. Krugman, P. R. (1979). Increasing returns, monopolistic competition, and international trade. *Journal of International Economics, 9*(4), 469–479.
27. Krugman, P. (1980). Scale economies, product differentiation, and the pattern of trade. *American Economic Review, 70*(5), 950–959.
28. Krugman, P. R. (1981). Intraindustry specialization and the gains from trade. *Journal of Political Economy, 89*(5), 959–973.
29. Laird, S. (1999). Regional trade agreements: Dangerous Liaisons? *The World Economy, 22*(9), 1179–1200.
30. Lakatos, C., & Nilsson, L. (2017). The EU-Korea FTA: Anticipation, trade policy uncertainty and impact. *Review of World Economics, 153*(1), 179–198.
31. Lancaster, K. (1980). Intra-industry trade under perfect monopolistic competition. *Journal of International Economics, 10*(2), 151–175.
32. Lee, H. (2001). General equilibrium evaluation of Japan-Singapore free trade agreement, ICSEAD, working paper Series, 2001–2023.
33. Lee, H.,Roland-Holst, D., & van der Mensbrugghe, D. (2001). General equilibrium assessments of trade liberalization in APEC countries. In M. Dutta et al. (Eds.), *Restructuring of Asian economies for the new millennium, 9B*.Amsterdam: Elsevier Science.
34. Loertscher, R., & Wolter, F. (1980). Determinants of intra-industry trade: Among countries and across industries. *Weltwirtschaftliches Archiv, 116*(2), 280–293.
35. Melitz, M. J. (2003). The impact of trade on intra-industry reallocations and aggregate industry productivity. *Econometrica, 71*(6), 1695–1725.
36. Nilsson, L. (2018). Reflections on the economic modelling of free trade agreements. *Journal of Global Economic Analysis, 3*(1), 156–186.
37. Norsten, C., & Burlutska, O. (2012). *Impact of the EU-South Korea free trade agreement on Swedish manufacturing firms School of Business, economics and law*. Göteborg: University of Gothenburg.
38. Raza, W., Grumiller, J., Taylor, L., Tröster, B., &von Arnim, R. (2014). Assess_TTIP: Assessing the claimed benefits of the transatlantic trade and investment partnership (TTIP), final report, Austrian foundation for development research.
39. Song, B.-H. (2015). Economic effects of the Japan-EU FTA and its influence on the Korean economy. *Korea Trade Review, 40*(3), 73–89.
40. Stolper, W. F., & Samuelson, P. A. (1941). Protection and real wages. *Review of Economic Studies, 9*(1), 58–73.
41. Yi, C. (2015). A study of ex post realized trade effects of Korea-EU FTA. *Journal of Korea Research Society for Customs, 16*(2), 321–344.
42. Yi, C. (2020). Brexit vote and Korea-EU trade structure, comparative advantage and intra-industry trade. *Korea International Trade Research Institute, 16*(1), 275–295.
43. Yi, C. (2009). An analysis of international trade structure between EU and Korea.*Journal of European Studies*.
44. Yi, C. (2012). An analysis of trade structure and comparative advantage of Busan area against EU, Korean.*Journal of European Studies,*1–42.
45. Zhai, F. (2008). Armington meets Melitz: Introducing firm heterogeneity in a global CGE model of trade. *Journal of Economic Integration, 23*(3), 575–604.

Chapter 4
A Discussion of the Japan-EU Economic Partnership Agreement: Negotiations, Tentative Results, and Potential

Masahiko Yoshii

Abstract The Japan-EU Economic Partnership Agreement (EPA)/Free Trade Agreement (FTA) was signed in July 2018 and came into effect in February 2019 after eighteen negotiation rounds beginning in April 2013. The agreement was initiated by the Japanese business circle, which was afraid of losing their competitiveness after the EU–Korea FTA went into effect. The Japanese business circle at first asked the EU to eliminate customs duties on their main export items like automobiles and electric appliances. On the other hand, the EU side asked Japan to eliminate or reduce non-tariff barriers to entry into the Japanese market and to accelerate exports of their agricultural products and foodstuff. Nearly one year has passed since the agreement went into force, and the first-hand statistical data shows positive results. Moreover, we can expect the agreement to extend its potential to upgrade the level of liberalization of other mega FTAs and facilitate the WTO reform. We must pay an attention to the implementation of the agreement, and expect the agreement to play more important roles in improving the global trade environment.

Keywords Japan-European EPA · Tariff elimination · Non-tariff barriers elimination · EU-Korea FTA · TTP

4.1 Introduction

The Japan-EU Economic Partnership Agreement (EPA) or Free Trade Agreement (FTA) was signed on 17 July 2018, and became effective on 1 February 2019. This agreement raised the economic relationship between Japan and the EU to a higher level. The Japan-EU EPA is not only the largest mega free trade agreement for both

M. Yoshii (✉)
Graduate School of Economics, Kobe University, 2-1 Rokkodai-cho,
Nada-ku, Kobe 657-8501, Japan
e-mail: yoshii@kobe-u.ac.jp

© Kobe University 2021   45
M. Yoshii and C.-D. Yi (eds.), *An Economic Analysis of Korea–EU FTA and Japan–EU EPA*, Kobe University Monograph Series in Social Science Research,
https://doi.org/10.1007/978-981-33-6145-4_4

economic regions, but will also serve as a high-level bridge to eliminate tariff and non-tariff barriers. Because Japan and the EU together account for 28% of global GDP and 37% of global trade, the agreement will also facilitate economic partnerships around the world.[1]

The first aim of this chapter is to summarise the conclusions of the Japan-EU EPA and introduce the immediate results, while the second aim is to consider the impacts of the Japan-EU EPA on negotiations of other FTAs and the World Trade Organisation (WTO) reform.

Section 2 summarises the economic relationships between Japan and the EU. The period of the 1970s and 1980s was called the 'trade friction era', but statistical data show that relationships have dramatically improved over the last twenty years. Section 3 describes what was negotiated in the Japan-EU EPA, and discusses its impacts on bilateral trade and the economies of Japan and the EU. Section 4 looks at the tentative results of the Japan-EU EPA and considers its impacts on negotiations of other mega FTAs and WTO reform. The last section concludes the discussion, asserting the importance of the Japan-EU EPA.

4.2   Economic Relationships Between Japan and the EU

4.2.1   Past Relationships[2]

In the history of economic relationships between Japan and the EU, the period of the 1970s and 1980s was called the trade friction era. Japanese exports to the EU, which consists of nine member countries, including the six original member countries,[3] the UK, Ireland, and Denmark, increased 3.5 times from 670 billion yen to 2.5 trillion yen in the 1970s, and the trade surplus increased by 16 times from 75.5 billion yen to 1.22 trillion yen. Notably, France recorded a trade surplus of 212.6 billion yen in 1970, but in 1977, the situation completely changed, resulting in a deficit of 1.27 trillion yen. The Japanese trade surplus further increased in the 1980s, finally reaching 3.96 trillion yen in 1992 (Fig. 4.1).

On the one hand, the EU imposed countermeasures against the Japanese 'unfair trade', such as quantitative import restrictions or anti-dumping customs duties, while Japan, on the other hand, lodged complaints with the GATT/WTO requesting the removal of these countermeasures. Additionally, to evade the anti-dumping measures, Japan used voluntary export restraints to limit her exports, especially of automobiles, to the EU and the US.

---

[1] https://www.mofa.go.jp/mofaj/files/000286927.pdf.

[2] This section's original paper is Yoshii ([24], 173–175).

[3] Belgium, France, Germany, Italy, Luxemburg, and Netherland.

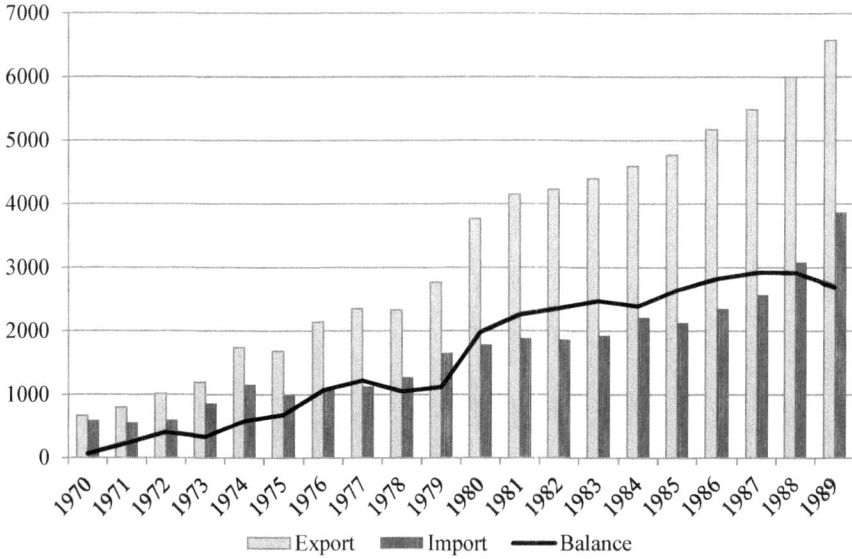

Fig. 4.1 Japanese trade with the EU 1970–1989 (trillion yen). *Source* Japan customs, trade statistics (https://www.customs.go.jp/toukei/suii/index.htm)

Japanese exports continued to increase later in the 1990s and 2000s, but the Japanese trade surpluses fluctuated between 2 and 4 trillion yen depending on the EU's economic situation, experiencing upswings during the EU's booms, and downswings during the slumps.

However, this situation has completely changed since the global financial crisis in 2009. Japanese exports to the EU dropped by 40% from 11.43 trillion yen in 2008 to 6.75 trillion yen in 2009, with the Japanese trade surplus also declining from 4.14 trillion yen to 1.23 trillion yen. Furthermore, the Japanese trade balance has shifted from surpluses to deficits since 2012. This shift was caused by the severe economic crisis in the Euro area, and the decline in export competitiveness of some important Japanese industrial products like electrical appliances. At this point, the trade friction era between Japan and the EU has ended (Fig. 4.2).

4.2.2   How Has Trade Between Japan and the EU Changed?

Next, we review how the trade of goods between Japan and the EU has changed over the last twenty years. First, we roughly review the kinds of goods that have been traded between Japan and the EU, because the composition of traded goods may have had different implications in the Japan-EU EPA negotiation.

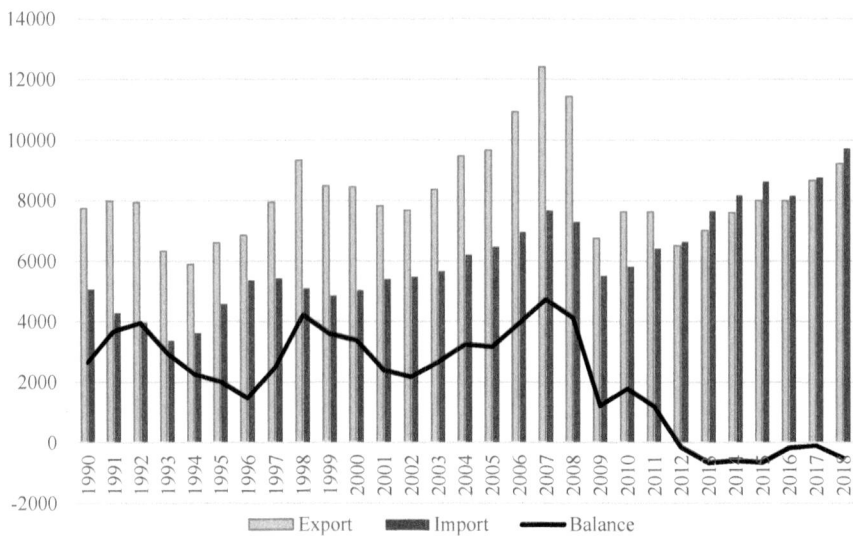

Fig. 4.2 Japanese trade with the EU 1990–2018 (trillion yen). *Source* Japan customs, trade statistics
(https://www.customs.go.jp/toukei/suii/index.html)

Table 4.1 shows the composition of Japanese exports to and imports from the EU
in terms of one-digit level standard industrial trade classification (SITC) codes. From
the Japanese export side, 70% has been concentrated in the machinery and transport
equipment sector (7), with the share of each of sectors 5, 6, 8, and 9 being around
10%; exports of sectors 0–4 have been negligibly small. The Japanese import side,

Table 4.1 Composition of Japanese exports to the EU (%)

SITC code		1990	1995	2000	2005	2010	2015
0	Food and animals	0.2	0.1	0.1	0.1	0.2	0.3
1	Beverages and tobacco	0.0	0.0	0.0	0.0	0.0	0.1
2	Crude materials, inedible	0.4	0.4	0.5	0.5	0.9	0.9
3	Mineral fuels	0.0	0.1	0.0	0.5	0.7	0.2
4	Animal & vegetable oil, fat	0.1	0.0	0.0	0.0	0.0	0.0
5	Chemicals	5.3	6.9	6.6	7.4	8.8	8.9
6	Manufactured goods	6.0	5.9	5.3	6.1	7.2	7.4
7	Machinery, transport equip	72.8	72.8	73.0	73.2	66.9	68.0
8	Miscellaneous articles	13.6	11.7	11.0	7.5	7.8	6.5
9	Commodities not classified	1.5	1.8	3.4	4.6	7.6	7.6
	Total	100	100	100	100	100	100

Source Calculated by the author from Japanese customs, trade statistics
(http://www.customs.go.jp/toukei/suii/html/time.htm)

Table 4.2 Composition of Japanese imports from the EU (%)

SITC code		1990	1995	2000	2005	2010	2015
0	Food and animals	4.9	5.9	6.5	6.4	5.7	6.0
1	Beverages and tobacco	4.0	3.3	3.1	3.1	5.7	3.6
2	Crude materials, inedible	2.3	3.0	3.1	3.1	2.8	2.2
3	Mineral fuels	0.5	0.1	0.2	0.2	0.4	0.6
4	Animal & vegetable oil, fat	0.1	0.2	0.4	0.4	0.4	0.6
5	Chemicals	14.8	19.3	24.1	24.1	31.5	32.5
6	Manufactured goods	12.8	11.3	9.0	9.0	7.6	6.5
7	Machinery, transport equip	33.0	36.7	36.0	36.0	31.1	33.9
8	Miscellaneous articles	24.9	18.0	16.5	16.5	13.9	13.4
9	Commodities not classified	2.6	2.1	1.3	1.3	0.9	0.8
	Total	100	100	100	100	100	100

Source Calculated by the author from Japan customs, trade statistics
(http://www.customs.go.jp/toukei/suii/html/time.htm)

however, presents a different picture (Table 4.2). Machinery and transport equipment has accounted for only about 35% of total imports, with the chemical sector (5) at same level as the present share, which grew from 15% in 1990 to more than 30% in the 2010s. By contrast, the share of the miscellaneous sector (9) has fallen by half, from 25 to 13%, over the last 25 years. Furthermore, the shares of the food and animals and beverages and tobacco sectors (0 and 1) still account for around 5%, in contrast with the Japanese export side.

Benz and Yalcin [2, pp. 4–5] used data from the OECD's STAN bilateral trade database to calculate the Grubel Lloyd (GL) index, and concluded that trade between Japan and the EU has a strong intra-industry nature.[4] We follow their approach and use similar data to calculate the GL index using Japanese trade statistics (Table 4.3). The data show that the manufacturing industries of Japan and the EU (sectors 5–8) have an intra-industrial nature, although the other industries (sectors 0–4) do not have these characteristics. Furthermore, the increase in the GL index of the machinery sectors for the last twenty years shows that the intra-industrial nature has become stronger, especially in the general and electrical machinery sectors.[5]

Next, we examine the composition of Japan-EU trade in more detail. Tables 4.4 and 4.5 show Japan's main export and import products based on the 3 to 5 digit SITC levels from 1990 to 2015. The list includes product items whose traded volumes

---

[4]$GLi = ((Xi + Mi) - |Xi - Mi|) / (Xi + Mi) = 1 - |Xi - Mi| / (Xi + Mi)$ with $0 \leq GLi \leq 1$, where X = exports and M = imports, i = industry. For GL close to 0, the respective Japanese industry merely exports or imports goods to/from the EU. For GL above 0.5, imports and exports in the respective industries are equivalent (for $GL = 1$, exports and imports are perfectly balanced) [2, p. 4]).

[5]Using the trade volume and number of trading products, Ando and Kimura [1] show that the extent and depth of production networks in Europe grew from that based on the simple WE (Western Europe)—CEE (Central and Eastern Europe) nexus to a global one with a strong connection to East Asia (including Japan), particularly in the electric machinery sector.

Table 4.3 GL index

SITC code		1990	1995	2000	2005	2010	2015
0	Food and animals	0.13	0.05	0.06	0.05	0.08	0.08
1	Beverages and tobacco	0.02	0.01	0.01	0.01	0.01	0.04
2	Crude materials, inedible	0.43	0.35	0.44	0.41	0.58	0.56
3	Mineral fuels	0.19	0.93	0.81	0.51	0.58	0.49
4	Animal & vegetable oil, fat	0.78	0.09	0.13	0.11	0.11	0.09
5	Chemicals	0.71	0.68	0.68	0.63	0.53	0.41
6	Manufactured goods	0.83	0.86	0.98	1.00	0.89	0.97
7	Machinery, transport equip	0.46	0.52	0.47	0.50	0.52	0.70
701	Machinery	0.43	0.46	0.46	0.50	0.50	0.67
703	Electrical machinery	0.24	0.36	0.38	0.43	0.52	0.65
705	Transport equipment	0.68	0.73	0.59	0.55	0.55	0.76
8	Miscellaneous articles	0.91	0.97	0.95	0.81	0.84	0.62
9	Commodities not classified	0.94	0.91	0.46	0.31	0.16	0.21

Data Calculated by the author from Japan customs, trade statistics
(https://www.customs.go.jp/toukei/suii/html/time.htm)

exceeded 200 billion yen in the case of Japanese exports and 100 billion yen in the case of imports.

On the Japanese export side, first, the listed main products have changed little, and all the listed product items except scientific and optical instruments (81101) and organic chemicals (50101) belong to the machinery sector (7), illustrating the concentration of Japanese exports to the EU in the machinery sector. Second, at the SITC 3-digit level, the most traded items have varied over time among machinery (701), electrical machinery (703), and transport equipment (705), but at the SITC 5-digit level, motor vehicles (70501) have always been the most important export sector. Third, in contrast to this dynamic transport equipment sector, electrical machinery has declined since the global financial crisis in 2009; its trade volume nearly halved from 2,563 billion in 2007, its peak, to 1,494 billion yen in 2015. Finally, the ratio of motor vehicle exports (70503) to motor vehicle parts exports (70505) has shrunk from 9.13 in 1990 to 2.55 in 2010 (2.92 in 2015), accounting for the development of assembly and parts producing networks in the EU area by Japanese automobile companies. As Fig. 4.3 shows, the share of the Central and Eastern European (CEE) countries has grown to almost 10% because of foreign direct investment (FDI) by Japanese automobile and electric appliance companies in the 2000s.[6]

---

[6]The assembly and parts producing networks cover not only the one in the EU countries, but also that in Russia. Because of the poor facilities of the Leningrad port, Toyota uses several ports in Finland and the Tallinn port in Estonia to transport a large volume of motor vehicle parts to its Leningrad assembly factory. In fact, export of motor vehicle parts (70,503) to Estonia, 6,872 million yen, was 16 times bigger than that to Latvia, 427 million yen, in 2015, and the export of motor vehicle parts per capita to Finland was 5,440 thousand yen that year.

Table 4.4 Main Japanese export products to the EU (million Yen)

1990			1995		
703	Electrical machinery	2,055,641	701	Machinery	1,796,475
70309	Visual apparatus	467,215	70101	Power generating machines	204,289
70311	Audio apparatus	321,309	7010505	Computers and units	549,366
70,323	Semiconductors and etc	295,576	7010507	Storage units	256,660
70,315	Telephony, telegraphy	208,717	703	Electrical machinery	1,617,572
701	Machinery	1,851,033	70323	Semiconductors and etc	423.237
7010505	Computers and units	569,981	70309	Visual apparatus	207,082
7,010,507	Storage units	232,602	705	Transport equipment	1,352,115
705	Transport equipment	1,727,131	70503	Motor vehicles	897,637
705503	Motor vehicles	1,332,663	70505	Parts of motor vehicles	225,815
70505	Parts of motor vehicles	146.007	81101	Scientific, optical inst	446,512
81101	Scientific, optical inst	570,614			
2000			**2005**		
703	Electrical machinery	2,322,190	701	Machinery	2,401,683
70323	Semiconductors and etc	523,186	7010507	Storage units	481,518
70309	Visual apparatus	431,110	70101	Power generating machines	409,833
701	Machinery	2,141,798	7010505	Computers and units	246,210
7010505	Computers and units	522,938	70125	Pump and centrifuges	222,673
701507	Storage units	312,069	705	Transport equipment	2,395,569
70101	Power generating machines	263,335	70503	Motor vehicles	1,634,290
705	Transport equipment	1,688,116	70505	Parts of motor vehicles	386,469

(continued)

Table 4.4 (continued)

1990			1995		
70503	Motor vehicles	952,915	7050701	Motorcycles, autocycles	265,466
7050701	Motorcycles, autocycles	251,937	703	Electrical machinery	2,272,477
70505	Parts of motor vehicles	251,055	70309	Visual apparatus	573,180
81101	Scientific, optical inst	558,714	70323	Semiconductors and etc	417,393
50101	Organic chemicals	210,370	70313	Audio apparatus	247,541
			81101	Scientific, optical inst	318,334
			50101	Organic chemicals	267,361
2010			**2015**		
701	Machinery	1,861,652	705	Transport equipment	1,974,898
7010507	Storage units	360,358	70503	Motor vehicles	1.240,659
70101	Power generating machines	352,333	70505	Parts of motor vehicles	425,070
70125	Pump and centrifuges	233,358	701	Machinery	1,964,271
705	Transport equipment	1,699,252	70101	Power generating machines	347,024
750503	Motor vehicles	1,016,219	70125	Pump and centrifuges	216,242
70505	Parts of motor vehicles	398,061	7010507	Storage units	273,050
703	Electrical machinery	1,536,125	703	Electrical machinery	1,494,289
70323	Semiconductors and etc	307,366	70327	Electrical measuring	264,382
70309	Visual apparatus	216,567	70323	Semiconductors and etc	200,487
81101	Scientific, optical inst	317,375	81101	Scientific, optical inst	265,043
50101	Organic chemicals	204,189	850101	Organic chemicals	205,649

Source Calculated by the author from Japan customs statistics
(http://www.customs.go.jp/toukei/html/time.htm)

Table 4.5 Main Japanese import products from the EU (million Yen)

1990			1995		
705	Transport equipment	896,762	705	Transport equipment	783,048
70501	Motor vehicles	783,924	70501	Motor vehicles	649,110
70503	Parts of motor vehicles	48,773	70503	Parts of motor vehicles	47,506
701	Machinery	501,941	701	Machinery	535,415
703	Electrical machinery	275,088	7010505	Computers and units	124,944
807	Clothing and accessories	259,342	703	Electrical machinery	361,108
50101	Organic chemicals	220,118	507	Medical products	286,952
611	Iron and steel products	213,790	507101	Organic chemicals	265,553
507	Medical products	196,557	807	Clothing and accessories	224,548
609	Textile yarn, fabrics	175,646	611	Iron and steel products	140,619
615	Manufactures of metals	112,152	609	Textile yarn, fabrics	120,264
805	Bags	105,756	805	Bags	110,186
			81101	Scientific, optical inst	108,246
2000			**2005**		
705	Transport equipment	707,120	705	Transport equipment	898,376
70501	Motor vehicles	586,697	70501	Motor vehicles	692,806
70503	Parts of motor vehicles	51,360	70503	Parts of motor vehicles	141,477
701	Machinery	639,730	701	Machinery	800,825
7010505	Computers and units	192,307	70101	Power generating machine	137,059
703	Electrical machinery	553,545	7010505	Computers and units	111,267
70307	Telephony, telegraphy	117,008	703	Electrical machinery	627,278
70311	Semiconductors etc	106,917	70313	Electrical measuring	153,235
50101	Organic chemicals	367,711	507	Medical products	550,542
507	Medical products	321,161	50101	Organic chemicals	483,946

(continued)

Table 4.5 (continued)

1990			1995		
81101	Scientific, optical inst	174,758	81,101	Scientific, optical inst	306,404
807	Clothing and accessories	159,055	805	Bags	180,073
003	Meat and meat preparation	153,303	003	Meat and meat preparation	178,335
805	Bags	137,672	807	Clothing and accessories	176,263
615	Nonferrous metals	109,960	611	Iron and steel products	118,995
611	Iron and steel products	102,513	615	Nonferrous metals	118,595
2010			**2015**		
507	Medical products	814,010	507	Medical products	1,714,096
705	Transport equipment	814,010	705	Transport equipment	1,199,298
70501	Motor vehicles	460,891	70501	Motor vehicles	899,753
70503	Parts of motor vehicles	122,329	70503	Parts of motor vehicles	144,229
701	Machinery	625,038	701	Machinery	988,255
70101	Power generating machine	154,292	70101	Power generating machine	298,423
703	Electrical machinery	539,254	703	Electrical machinery	726,808
70313	Electrical measuring	116,354	70313	Electrical measuring	178,506
50101	Organic chemicals	530,350	50101	Organic chemicals	483,741
81101	Scientific, optical inst	295,387	81101	Scientific, optical inst	383,514
805	Bags	126,669	805	Bags	185,644
003	Meat and meat preparation	121,353	807	Clothing and accessories	168,718
615	Manufactures of metals	110,053	003	Meat and meat preparation	165,717

Source Calculated by the author from Japan customs, trade statistics
(https://www.customs.go.jp/toukei/suii/html/time.htm)

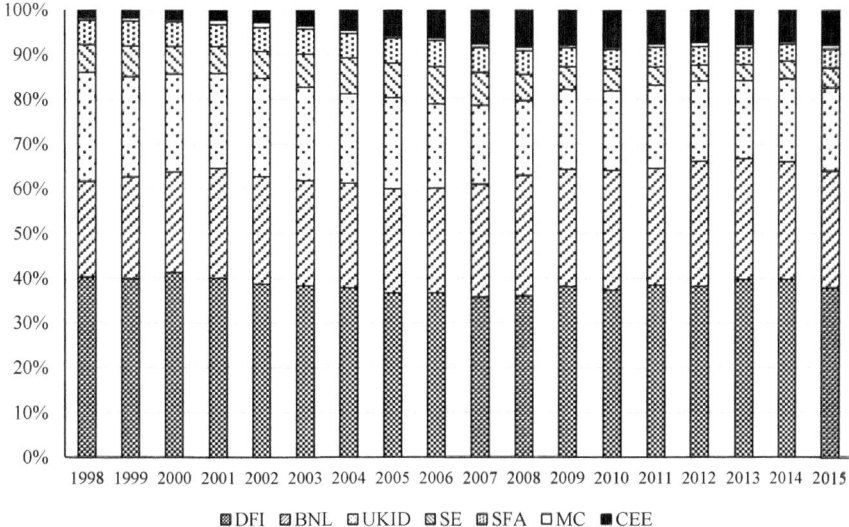

Fig. 4.3 Japanese exports to the EU by country groupings. *Source* Japan custums, trade statistics (http://www.customs.go.jp/toukei/srch/index.htm?M-23&P=0)

On the Japanese import side, the picture is substantially different. First, Japanese import items have not been limited to machinery (7). Such miscellaneous articles as bags (805) and clothing and accessories (807), as well as meat and meat preparation (003), are listed as main import products. Second, the volume of medical products (507) imports has increased by 8.7 times from 196 billion yen in 1990 to 1,714 billion yen, and now is the most important item imported in Japan. Third, the ratio of motor vehicle imports to motor vehicle parts imports is relatively higher than that in the Japanese export case, although the ratio itself decreased from 16.1 in 1990 to 3.8 in 2010 (6.2 in 2015). The difference can be explained by the fact that European automobile companies do not have any assembly factories in Japan (Fig. 4.4).

4.3 The Japan-EU EPA Negotiation[7]

4.3.1 Background of the Japan-EU EPA

Negotiation of the Japan-EU EPA was instigated by private Japanese initiatives. The Japan Business Federation, *Keidanren*, published the 'Basic View of the European Integration and the Japan-European Economic Relationships' (in Japanese)[8]

---

[7]This section's original paper is [24, 18–19].

[8]https://www.keidanren.or.jp/japanese/policy/2006/017.html.

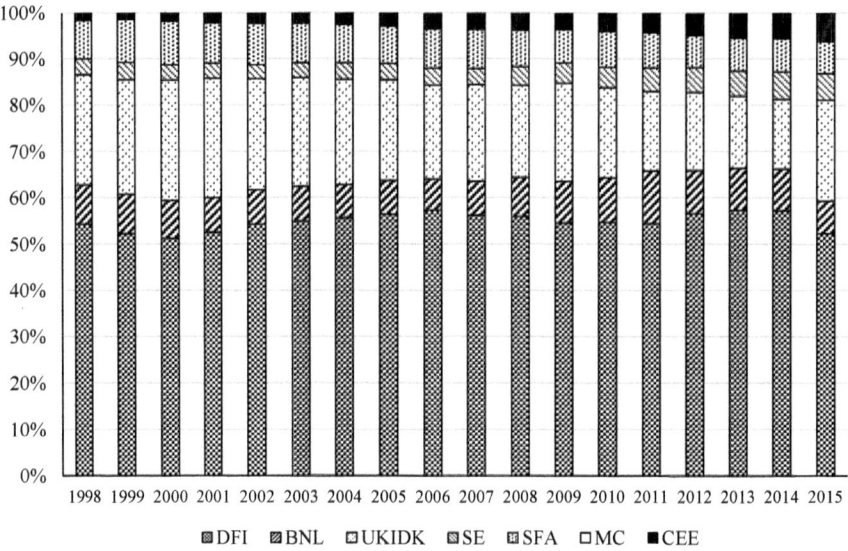

Fig. 4.4 Japanese imports from the EU by country groupings. *Source* Japan customs, trade statistics.
https://www.customs.go.jp/toukei/srch/index.htm?M=23&P=0/

in April 2006, saying that 'Japan should enhance her bilateral economic relationships with each European country, taking the EPA into consideration.' At the Japan-EU BDRT (Business Dialogue Round Table) held in Berlin in June 2007, Japanese and European business leaders proposed that 'Japan and the EU authorities should establish a task force with business support to explore the feasibility of a Japan-EU Economic Integration Agreement, which should be an enriched economic agreement that includes priority issues for business like strengthened regulatory cooperation, intellectual property, trade enhancement, and an improved investment environment.'[9] *Keidanren* also published a memorandum 'Request to initiate a joint study on the Japan-EU EPA' (in Japanese).[10] The task force was launched with the JETRO (Japan External Trade Organization) as its headquarters, publishing an interim report in February 2008, and the 'Report by the Japan-EU Economic Integration Agreement (EIA) Study Group' in September 2009.[11]

Why was the Japanese side eager to start the EPA/FTA negotiation, while the EU side was not? The reason is because Japanese customs tariffs on most manufacturing products are set at close to zero per cent, but the EU levies high tariffs on sensitive manufacturing products. For example, the EU levies a 10% tariff on automobiles, and a 14% tariff on liquid crystal and plasma displays, and the European business communities have opposed eliminating these tariffs. Therefore, in the position paper for the first meeting with the Japanese task force group in March 2008, the EU side proposed

---

[9]https://www.eu-japan-brt.eu/sites/eu-japan-brt.eu/files/joint_recommendations_june07_0.pdf.

[10]https://www.keidanren.or.jp/japanese/policy/2007/050.html.

[11]https://www.jetro.go.jp/ext_images/jfile/report/07000103/eu_eia.pdf.

including various issues such as the curtailment of Japanese import restrictions on agricultural products, deregulation to increase service trade, and further liberalization of the government procurement market.[12] The differences in their interests became clearer, as Japan requested the reduction and/or elimination of import customs tariffs on manufacturing products to the EU, and the EU requested elimination of non-tariff barriers (NTB) and opening of the Japanese government procurement market.

To respond to these requests from the EU side, *Keidanren* published two papers: 'Toward the realization of Japan-EU Economic Integration: the Second Proposal for the Japan-EU EPA' in April 2009[13] and 'Requests to initiate the Japan-EU EPA Negotiation: the Third Proposal for the Japan-EU EPA' in July 2009.[14] Furthermore, *Keidanren* announced a joint statement with the European Business Council, 'The Regular Japan-EU Summit Meeting: the EIA Negotiation should Start Now' in April 2010,[15] to strongly appeal to both Japan and the EU to start EPA negotiations.

Consequently, the Japan-EU regular summit in April 2010 established a 'Joint High Level Group (JHLG)' of vice-ministerial officials of both sides to begin a meaningful negotiation. At the next Japan-EU regular summit in May 2011, Japan and the EU agreed to start the process of parallel negotiations for a deep and comprehensive FTA/EPA, addressing all issues of shared interests of both sides, including tariffs, non-tariff measures, services, investment, intellectual property rights, competition, and public procurement, and a binding agreement covering political, global, and other sectoral cooperation in a comprehensive manner, underpinned by their shared commitment to fundamental values and principles.[16] To this end, the summit determined that the two sides would initiate discussions with a view towards defining the scope and level of ambition of both negotiations.[17]

After the scoping discussion, in July 2012, the European Commission asked the European Council for negotiating authority, and consent was given by the Foreign Affairs Council in July 2012. Finally, the Japan-EU telephone summit conference in March 2013 officially decided to start the Japan-EU EPA negotiation.

The reason the road to beginning the Japan-EU EPA negotiation was accelerated in the 2010s is that the EU-Korea FTA came into effect in July 2011. The Japanese side was seriously concerned that Japan would lose its competitiveness in the EU market, and hurried to start the negotiation by making concessions to the EU such as relaxation of regulations regarding the location of auto-repair shops in housing areas, and the change in regulations on engines of imported sports cars.[18] The motivation for the EU side was much weaker. However, Prime Minister Kan's keynote speech at the House of Representatives in October 2010, indicating that Japan would consider participating in the Trans-Pacifice Partnership (TPP) negotiation, and the Tohoku

---

[12]Watanabe ([21], 33).

[13]https://www.keidanren.or.jp/japanese/policy/2009/037/honbun.pdf.

[14]https://www.keidanren.or.jp/japanese/policy/2009/099/honbun.pdf.

[15]https://www.keidanren.or.jp/japanese/policy/2010/036.pdf.

[16]https://www.mofa.go.jp/region/europe/eu/summit/overview1106.html.

[17]https://www.mofa.go.jp/region/europe/eu/joint1105.html.

[18]Watanabe (2014, 36).

Region Pacific Coast Earthquake in March, 2011 might have given the EU side motivation to start the Japan-EU EPA negotiation.

The first round of the negotiation was held in Brussels in April 2013, and thereafter, eighteen rounds of negotiations were held. At the Japan-EU summit in May 2015, both leaders agreed to further accelerate the negotiation, aiming to reach an agreement in principle during 2015.[19] The agreement was signed on 17 July 2018, and came into effect on 1 February 2019.

4.3.2   What Was Negotiated?[20]

It was hard to acquire knowledge of the detailed contents of the negotiation, as the press releases revealed only a summary of the negotiation, and the attention of the mass media was so low that the contents were rarely reported.[21] The Japanese Ministry of Foreign Affairs' website only mentioned the following areas of interest[22]:
   Japan's main areas of interest are:

– The elimination of high tariffs on industrial products (e.g. motor cars, 10%; electrical machinery, 14% at the highest) to improve competitive conditions for Japanese products in the European market, and.
– Regulatory issues facing Japanese companies in Europe.

   The EU's main areas of interest are:

– Non-tariff measures (NTMs) on automobiles, chemicals, electrical machinery, food safety, processed food, medical devices, and pharmaceuticals, among others;
– Government procurement (e.g. railways); and.
– Elimination of tariffs on the main products exported to Japan.

   The website of the Delegation of the European Union in Japan only summarised the main negotiation areas, without referring to any concrete negotiating points[23]:
   The negotiations took place in Working Groups which covered the following areas: Trade in goods (including Market Access, General Rules, Trade Remedies, Industrial goods), Technical Barriers to Trade and Non-Tariff Measures, Rules of Origin, Customs and Trade Facilitation, Sanitary and Phytosanitary Measures, Trade in Services, Investment, Procurement, Intellectual Property, Competition Policy, Trade and Sustainable Development, Other issues (General and Regulatory Cooperation,

---

[19] https://www.mofa.go.jp/files/000013835.pdf.

[20] This section's original paper is [24, 22–25].

[21] We checked the number of articles on the Nikkei (Japan Economic Daily) from 1 January 2013 to 31 July 2016 using the Nikkei Telecom (database service provided by the Nikkei). There are only 187 articles concerning the Japan-EU EPA, although there are 6,725 articles on TPP.

[22] https://www.mofa.go.jp/files/000013835.pdf.

[23] https://www.euinjapan.jp/en/relations/trade/.

Corporate Governance and Business Environment, Electronic Commerce, Animal Welfare) and Dispute Settlement.

Before reaching the agreement in general in 2017, three reports were published from the EU perspective—the EU Report, 2009; EU Report, 2012; and EU Report, 2015—and one report from the Japanese side [19], through which we can obtain a glimpse of the concrete negotiating points, and what was negotiated. We should, however, note that these four reports generally described non-tariff barriers very well, but touched only briefly on the elimination and reduction of tariff barriers.

Among the four reports, the EU Report, 2012 had the most important role, as it was edited by the European Commission when both sides decided to start the negotiation. We also identify important topics from the EU Report, 2015, as it described the negotiation points in detail. We summarize them in such sectors as automobiles, foodstuff, pharmaceuticals, government procurement, and others, especially paying attention to NTBs.

(1) Motor vehicles[24]

Within the long history of Japan-EU trade talks, motor vehicles have been the most hotly negotiated area since the 1970s; however, this tension is becoming relatively more relaxed.

First, as seen in the previous section, after the severe trade frictions in the 1970s and 1980s, Japanese automobile companies steadily increased their local production in the EU area, although European automobile companies do not produce any cars in Japan.

Second, because of the increase in local production by Japanese automobile companies, the motor vehicle trade between Japan and the EU is now more or less balanced. European cars account for 80% of Japanese motor vehicle imports, but Japanese cars account for only 20% of EU motor vehicle imports. Furthermore, Korean automobile makers have increased their share of the EU market, while EU imports of Japanese motor vehicles have decreased by 35% over the last five years.

The EU Report, 2015 summarised the quite different results in the four reports about the effect of tariff reduction on the motor vehicle trade between Japan and the EU.[25] The EU Report, 2009 predicted the tariff reduction would increase EU exports by 13% and Japanese exports by 56%. However, the EU Report, 2012 predicted a much smaller tariff reduction effect: a 5% increase in Japanese exports and a 0.1% increase in EU exports. The EU Report, 2015 noted that the EU Report, 2012 gave the most realistic estimation.

Among the negotiation agendas on motor vehicle trade, NTBs as well as tariff reductions were also important topics:

---

[24]EU Report [7, 113–126].

[25]Francoi, Manchin, Norberg, *Economic Impact Assessment of an FTA between the EU and Japan*, 2011; Deloitte Belgium, *EU-Japan Free Trade Agreement: Impact Assessment on the Automotive Industry*, 2012; Mitsubishi Research Institute, *Assessment of the Impact on the Automobile Market of an EU-Japan Economic Integration Agreement (EIA)*, 2012; and Copenhagen Economics, *The Impact of Trade Liberalisation on the EU Automotive Industry: Trends and Prospects*, 2014.

- vehicle regulations: Both the EU and Japan are signatories of the United Nations Economic Commission for Europe (UNECE) 1958 Agreement concerning the Adoption of Uniform Technical Prescriptions. However, as Japan had unilaterally adopted 40 passenger vehicle regulations, the outstanding regulations were likely discussed in the FTA negotiations;
- measurement of emissions and fuel efficiency: harmonising test-driving cycles;
- zoning issues for dealerships and auto-servicing shops[26];
- '*kei* car': Japan has its own vehicle category, the '*kei* car', with an engine size of no more than 660 cc, and it gives tax, insurance, and registration preferences to this type of vehicle. EU manufacturers have been afraid that they are effectively locked out of a huge chunk of the Japanese market, and requested the removal of these preferences. The EU Report, 2015 made a cost comparison, and concluded that 58% of the difference between the total costs of owning a 'kei car' and an imported small car is explained by the difference in average purchase price, 31% by the difference in taxes and insurance, and 11% by fuel consumption;
- exchange rate fluctuations: for the last few years, JPY/EUR exchange rates have fluctuated in a wider range than JPY/USD or JPY/SDR exchange rates, and have a bigger impact on competitiveness than tariff liberalization; and.
- new market challenges: connectivity and the smart car concept, leading to competition from new entrants, would completely change regulatory barriers.

(2) Food[27]

Although Japan is a large importer of beef, 95% of Japanese imports come from Canada, the US, Chile, Australia, and New Zealand. The farm gate unit value of beef production is estimated to be roughly 9,200 USD per ton in Japan, which is almost twice the farm gate price in the EU (4,800 USD per ton). However, the farm gate prices in the US (4,600 USD per ton) and Australia (2,700 USD per ton) are even lower, and the ban on beef imports imposed by Japan following the BSE crisis in Europe continues to have a negative impact on beef imports from the EU. Thus, European beef producers should not only request a reduction in tariffs on beef but overcome the handicap of the BSE safety issue that exists in the minds of Japanese consumers.

Unlike the beef case, Japan is a substantial export market for EU pork producers, since its imports from the EU amount to 23% of all Japanese pork imports. The EU Report, 2015 noted that Japanese protection is much more sophisticated and distortive in the pork case than in the beef case, and the impact of total liberalization of the Japanese pork market would be difficult to estimate.

In contrast to the beef and pork cases, the daily products sector is one where the EU may have greater competitiveness. For example, Japan's farm gate price of

---

[26]'Japan relaxed a regulation on the location permission of auto-servicing shops in housing areas so that import car dealers might have less difficulty in establishing auto-servicing shops.' (Watanabe (2014, 36)).

[27]EU Report [7, 133–146].

raw milk, 0.91 USD per kg, is roughly twice the EU average farm gate price, 0.45 USD per kg. However, the EU's share of Japanese imports of daily products is only 20%, because of its very sophisticated and high protection[28] and difficulty competing with other main producers, such as Australia, New Zealand, and the US, which, as a whole, account for 65% of Japanese daily products imports.

Among daily products, the EU may have much stronger competitiveness in cheese products, because the Japanese protection system is much simpler. As the EU share of Japanese daily products imports remains at 27% for various reasons,[29] the EU strongly requests concessions from Japan on cheese products.

(3) Pharmaceuticals and medical devices[30]

As seen in Sect. 2.2, pharmaceuticals and medical devices are currently the biggest export items from the EU to Japan, and the sector is the most important for the EU in terms of its output volume and number of employees. Therefore, liberalization of Japanese NTBs in this sector was one of the most hotly debated topics in the Japan-EU EPA negotiation.

While both the EU and Japan are signatories of the WTO plurilateral agreement on pharmaceutical products, and the EU-Japan Mutual Recognition Agreements entered into force in 2002, the EU Report, 2015 pointed out the following unsolved NTBs in the pharmaceutical and medical devices sector:

– the approval and introduction of new medicines is delayed for two to three years because of the complex regulatory environment,
– the introduction of new and innovative medicines is hindered because of non-transparent price and reimbursement rules,
– there are additional requirements for the introduction of new medical devices because of restrictive safety standards, and.
– the slow submission and approval procedures for medical devices results in higher approval and production costs.

The EU Report, 2015 reported that regulatory convergence is important, as these disincentive measures imply additional costs corresponding to a 22% tariff on pharmaceutical products and a 30% tariff on medical devices. For this purpose, the Japan-Switzerland EPA/FTA is a successful precedent, as the agreement grants up to five years of compensation in cases of significant market delays due to lengthy authorization procedures for innovative pharmaceutical and plant protection products.

---

[28] Yamashita [22] explains how the Japanese raw milk market is distorted by the milk supply system, which is controlled by the government and monopolized by the Hokuren, Hokkaido Association of Agricultural Cooperatives.

[29] The EU Report [8, 142–143] lists four other reasons: cheese products are the most important source of EU exports; profitability is higher; the gains in trade from cutting ad valorem tariffs are more straightforward; and the preferences granted to Australia are larger for cheese products.

[30] EU Report [7, 147–156].

(4) Government procurement

The EU strongly requests that Japan open its government procurement markets. Japan is a signatory to the WTO Government Procurement Agreement (GPA), and has steadily opened its procurement markets. The EU, however, claims that the level of Japanese procurement transparency and non-discrimination is not as high as that in the EU procurement market. First, there are different legal bases for procurement at the central government and prefecture levels, and no consolidated English language information. The EU requests that Japan establish a central electronic information source in English so that even EU small and medium enterprises (SMEs) could penetrate the Japanese procurement market. Second, in the Japanese procurement market, the EU Report, 2015 points out *de facto* preferences are likely to be more important than *de jure* preferences. The Japanese government needs to address the *de facto* preferences through enhanced transparency measures. Third, the EU requests Japan, as a signatory to the GPA, to enlarge coverage of the procurement units of 19 designated cities as well as 47 prefectures. Moreover, the EU requests reducing the thresholds of work contracts for the sub-central procurement level from today's 15 million SDR to the 5 million SDR that is used in the EU and is the norm in most procurements covered by the GPA.[31]

As Japan's Ministry of Foreign Affairs' website shows, the public procurement sector the EU is most interested in is the railway sector.[32] The passenger-kilometres (PK) of the East Japan Railway (JR East) alone, 126,960 billion PK, is more than that of the entire German railway network, 88,064 billion PK, but total imports in the rail supply industry in Japan were only 200 million Euros in 2009, accounting for just 6.3% of domestic production, 3.1 billion Euros. The EU Report, 2015 did not directly demand opening of the procurement markets of the Japanese railway networks, especially JRs, but, recommended rail suppliers in Japan and the EU cooperate in the very dynamic third markets to enhance Japan-EU industrial cooperation.[33]

(5) Other topic areas.

The core negotiation topics of the Japan-EU EPA are, of course, in tariffs and NTBs. However, we should note some other important negotiation areas of social, human rights, and environmental significance. Next, we summarise interesting topics in the labour area.

The most important aspect of the Japan-EU EPA is its impact on the labour markets. For example, there are concerns that eliminating or gradually reducing the EU's tariff on motor vehicles could increase motor vehicle imports from

---

[31] EU Report [7, 34–35].

[32] All the JR companies were listed in Annex 3 of Japan in Appendix 1 of the WTO GPA (https://www.wto.org/english/tratop_e/gproc_e/jpn3.doc) which was signed in 1994. Note, first, that note 4 (a) to Annex3 says that procurement related to operational safety of transportation is not included. Second, after their hundred per cent privatization, three JRs on the Main Island (JR East, JR Central, and JR West) were excluded from the list as of 28 October 2014.

[33] EU Report [7, 127–130].

Table 4.6 Summary of tariff elimination

		Item/line no	Volume	Item/line no	Volume
Industrial products	Japan	96.3	81.7	100	100
	EU	96.0	96.2	100	100
Agricultural products	Japan	54		82	
	EU	95		98	

Source JETRO [14, p. 8]

Japan, and have a negative impact on employment in the European motor vehicles industry. Regarding this concern, the EU Report, 2012 reported that eliminating the EU's tariff on motor vehicles might, on the contrary, further increase direct investment of Japanese automobile companies, because they now have 13 assembly factories and 5 research centres in the EU area.[34]

There are, however, some tasks other than securing employment that Japan is expected to accomplish. All the EU member states have ratified all eight International Labour Organisation (ILO) Fundamental Conventions, but Japan has not ratified the two conventions dealing with non-discrimination (Convention 111) and the abolition of forced labour (Convention 105). Both the EU and ILO have asked the Japanese government to take immediate and concrete measures to arrange the legislative framework.[35]

Furthermore, the EU, following the features identified in the EU-Korea and EU-Canada FTAs, requests Japan organise a Domestic Advisory Group and a Civil Society Forum to facilitate ratification of the ILO Fundamental Conventions and the Decent Work Agenda, and to monitor their implementation.

4.3.3 What Was Concluded?

The Japan-EU EPA was signed in July 2018, and became effective in February 2019. The agreement comprised 23 chapters, a larger number than in the EU-Korea FTA (see Chapter 3 and [13]).

The agreed elimination of customs duties is summarised in Table 4.6. More than 90% of the EU's exports to Japan will be duty free once the agreement takes effect. Once the agreement is fully implemented, Japan will have scrapped customs duties on 97% of the goods imported from the EU (in tariff lines), with the remaining tariff lines being subject to partial liberalisation through tariff rate quotas or tariff reductions.[36] The general level of tariff elimination is very close to that of another Japanese mega FTA, the Trans-Pacific Partnership Agreement (TPP) 11, which went into effect in December 2018 [15].

---

[34]EU Report [6, 49–50].

[35]EU Report [7, 61–62].

[36]https://ec.europa.eu/commission/news/eu-japan-trade-agreement-enters-force-2019-feb-01_en.

In terms of the most controversial issue of eliminating tariffs and NTBs on automobile trade, the EU will eliminate customs tariffs on automobiles in eight years, their parts in at most nine years, and on electric appliances in six years. Japan will also strengthen her efforts toward harmonisation and mutual recognition of Japanese automobile safety regulations with the World Forum for Harmonizing Vehicle Regulations and UNECE regulations.

Regarding agricultural products and foodstuffs, we should mention that Japan successfully maintained the protection level of the five most important agricultural products—rice, wheat, beef and pork meat, dairy products, and sugar cane—at the same level as TPP or TPP11. Japan did concede in eliminating or reducing tariff and NTBs on many other agricultural products and foodstuffs. Both Japan and the EU instantly eliminated customs duties on wine, and Japan will eliminate tariffs on pasta, chocolates, and leader products in 11 years, and reduce tariffs on cheese with bigger margins than in the case of TPP11.

Concerning paratheatrical products, Japan seems not to have given significant concessions to the EU. In the case of public procurement, Japan enlarged the scope of application by adding to the list sub-central government entities, local independent administrative agencies, and sub-central government entities who produce, transport, or distribute electricity. In addition, the Japanese side abolished a safe explanatory note for the railway sector to allow European railway cargo producers to penetrate the Japanese market.

The Japan-EU EPA also adopted various non-tariff measures as well as tariff measures on traded goods and services to upgrade the bilateral economic relationships. The geographical indication (GI) system is an example. By introducing the European GI system to Japan as well as introducing the Japanese GI system to the EU market, producers of GI products, like French wine with *Appellation d'Origine Controlee* (AOC), Kobe beef, and so on, can protect their products in the other party's market.

4.3.4   Economic Impacts of the Japan-EU EPA

In addition to economic researchers, the EU and Japanese governments themselves estimated the economic impacts of the Japan-EU EPA. Among these results, the EU report, 2009 and EU Report, 2012 are early examples. The Japanese government also published [4] to illustrate the positive results of the Japan-EU EPA.[37] The European Parliament [10] summarised some of these estimations, which in general demonstrate the positive impacts on the EU economy, and show the worth of the Japan-EU EPA. Interestingly, while later results showed positive signs, early estimations showed negative impacts of the Japan-EU EPA on the EU GDP, which reminds us that the

---

[37] The Cabinet Office [4] concluded that the Japan-EU EPA would increase Japanese GDP by almost 1 percentage point (5.2 trillion yen) and the number of employees by 292 thousand.

EU side responded negatively to the Japan-EU EPA before negotiations were initiated (Table 4.7).

Finally, we summarise the two latest studies, [11, 12], which also show the Japan-EU EPA's positive impacts on both parties. However, we should be aware that the

Table 4.7 Comparison of simulation results

Stduy	"GDP (in % Change)"	Bilateral trade (in % change)	Employment (in % change)	Real wages (in % change)
European Coommission (2018)	Increase in EU GDP by EUR 34 billion (+0.14%)	EU export to Japan increase by 13.2% EU import from Japan increase by 23.5%	n.a	n.a
Vicard [20]	Increase by + 0.07% in EU's GDP per capita	EU goods trade with Japan inreases by + 0.5% (in weighted average) for a GDP increase of 0.1%	n.a	n.a
Ifo Working Paper (2018)	Long-run real income increases by USD 15bn. (+0.10%) for EU, similar across all scenarios	EU exports to Japan increase by 73% (USD83bn.) and EU imports from Japan increase by 63% (USD79bn.)	Ifo Trade Model holds total employment constant, only allows for labour reallocation across sectors	n.a
Ifo Study (2017)	Average change for the EU-28 is + 0.06%	EU exports increase by 61% and EU imports increase by 55%	Ifo Trade Model holds total employment constant, only allows for labour reallocation across sectors	n.a
TSIA [8]	Long term impact for EU's GDP is + 0.76%	+ 34% for the EU and + 29% for Japan	Adjust CIAR results by + 192,000 jobs in manufacturing and services sectors	low skilled: 0.68% high skilled: 0.70%"
Benz and Yalcin [2]	0.21%	EU exports increas by 4.2% and EU imports from Japan inrease by 11%		

(continued)

Table 4.7 (continued)

Stduy	"GDP (in % Change)"	Bilateral trade (in % change)	Employment (in % change)	Real wages (in % change)
Copenhagen Economics (2010)	+ 0.10 to 0.14%	EU exports to Japan + 46–71% of EU's 2008 baseline EU imports from Japan + 40–61% of Japan's baseline exports to the EU in 2008	n.a	
Ecorys (2009)	−0.1% for EU26	EU26 exports to Japan + 0.4% EU26 imports from Japan + 0.4%"	Low skilled: −7.8% High skilled: −7.8%"	Low skilled: 0.1% High skilled: 0.1%"
Swedish National Board of Trade (2009)	−0.01%	Trade flows increase by 34%	n.a	n.a

Source European parliament [10, pp. 53–54]

impact on the Japanese economy is larger than the impact on the EU economy, because of the difference in trade shares between Japanese exports to the EU and EU exports to Japan. Moreover, [12] show that, under the Japan-EU EPA, a soft Brexit scenario would have better result for Japan than hard Brexit, but once the Japan-EU EPA is implemented, there would not be any significant differences for the EU economy between a soft Brexit and hard Brexit (Tables 4.8 and 4.9).

Table 4.8 Macroeconomic impact of the EU-Japan EPA in 2035 (% and billion euro)

	EU		Japan	
	%	Billion euro	%	Billion euro
GDP	0.14	33.874	0.61	29.066
Bilateral exports	13.2	13,541	23.5	22,215

Source EU [11, p. 49]

Table 4.9 Real income changes, in %

	Soft brexit scenario	Hard brexit scenario
Japan	0.31	0.27
UK	0.11	0.10
R of EU	0.10	0.10
Germany	0.08	0.08
France	0.07	0.07
Italy	0.06	0.06

Source Felbermayr et al. [12, p. 119]

4.4   Tentative Results of the Japan-EU EPA

4.4.1   General Trend

As only eleven months have passed since enforcement of the Japan-EU EPA began in February 2019, we can only tentatively test whether there are any differences in trade between Japan and the EU before and after enforcement.

Figures 4.5 and 4.6 show the monthly data of Japanese exports to and imports from the EU between 2017 and 2019. According to the graphs, which show that neither exports nor imports in 2019 clearly surpassed the 2017 and 2018 results, we cannot say that the Japan-EU EPA has yet produced positive results in the trade volume between Japan and the EU.

Next, we confirm whether the Japan-EU EPA has increased the share of Japanese exports to and imports from the EU in total Japanese trade by conducting a two-sided t-test of the average shares before and after EPA enforcement. According to the t-test, the share of Japanese exports to the EU significantly differs after the enforcement

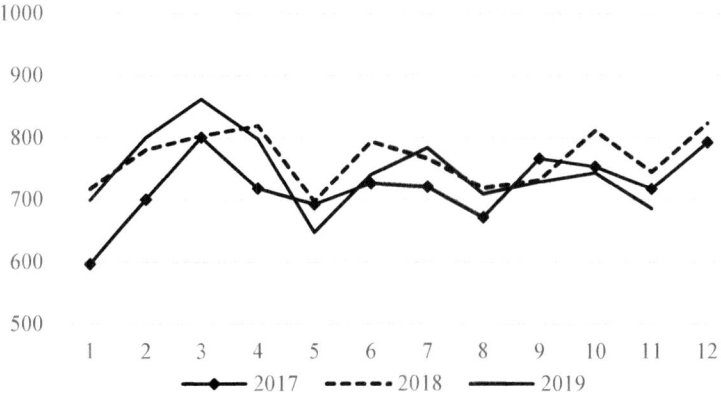

Fig. 4.5 Japanese export to the EU (trillion yen). *Source* Japan customs, trade statistics (https://www.customs.go.jp/toukei/suii/index.htm)

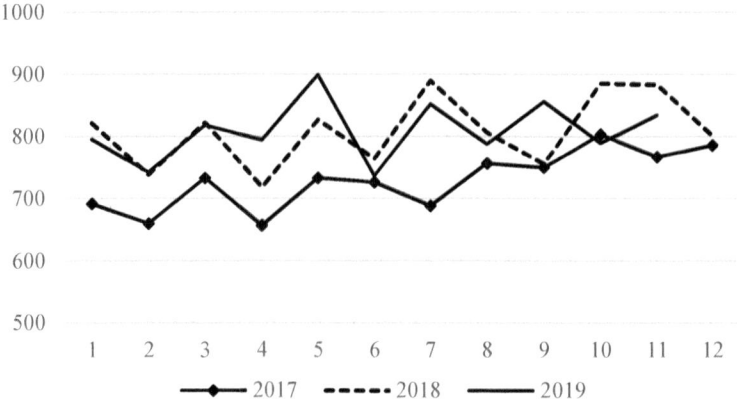

Fig. 4.6 Japanese import from the EU (trillion yen). *Source* Japan customs, trade statistics (https://www.customs.go.jp/toukei/suii/index.htm)

Table 4.10 Average of Japanese exports		Before	After
	Average	11.243	11.567
	Distribution	0.254	0.267
	No. of observations	25	10
	t-value	−1.708	
	p-value	0.097	

Source Own calculation

(at the 10% significance level), and the share of Japanese imports from the EU also significantly differs after the enforcement (at the 5% significance level). We can tentatively say that the Japan-EU EPA has produced a positive result for trade between Japan and the EU (Tables 4.10 and 4.11).

Table 4.11 Average of Japanese imports		Before	After
	Average	11.681	12.507
	Distribution	0.263	0.197
	No. of observations	25	10
	t-value	−4.464	
	p-value	0.086	

Source Own calculation

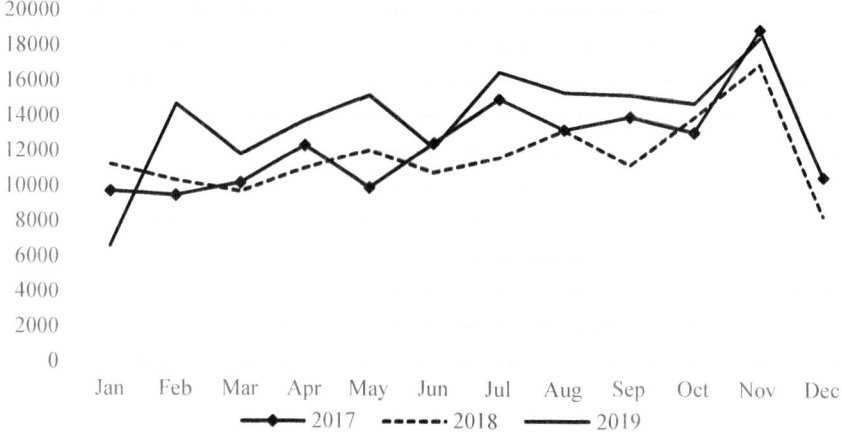

Fig. 4.7 Japanese wine import from EU (KL). *Source* Japan customs, trade statistics (https://www.customs.go.jp/toukei/suii/index.htm)

4.4.2 Japanese Wine Imports from the EU

The most successful example of the Japan-EU EPA is Japanese imports of wine from the EU. Before enforcement of the Japan-EU EPA, Japan imposed a customs tariff of 67–125 yen per litre on imported bottles of wine, and the EU also imposed a customs tariff of 0.154 euros per litre on imported bottles of wine. Both parties immediately eliminated the tariffs on the enforcement date. Figure 4.7 shows that Japanese imports of wine from the EU in 2019 exceeded the imported volume in 2017 and 2018, although wine importers restrained from importing wine in January, 2019.

Besides eliminating wine import tariffs, NTMs such as introduction of the geographical indication (GI) system and relaxation of ingredients and additives regulations were implemented. Such non-tariff measures should contribute to increasing the wine trade between Japan and the EU.[38]

4.4.3 Impacts on Other FTA Negotiations and the WTO Reform

Impacts of the Japan-EU EPA on Other Mega FTAs

The fact that two large economic regions, Japan and the EU, concluded an EPA/FTA with a high level of tariff and NTB reduction will have a spill-over effect on other mega FTA negotiations. On the one hand, Japan is negotiating the Japan–China-South

---

[38] https://www.customs.go.jp/kyotsu/kokusai/news/eu_siryou.pdf.

Korea and Regional Comprehensive Economic Partnership (RCEP) with ASEAN10, China, South Korea, Australia, New Zealand, and India.[39] On the other hand, the EU is negotiating FTAs with developed countries such as the US (TTIP), Australia, and New Zealand, and with developing countries, such as those in Latin America, and American countries are negotiating with the Asian countries of ASEAN, India, and China (investment agreement).

It is said that the tariff concession rates of FTAs with developing countries are relatively low, sometimes less than ninety per cent, which corresponds to the threshold of 'the duties and other restrictive regulations of commerce are eliminated on substantially all trade' of article 24–8(b) of the WTO treaty. For example, [17, p. 2] said that the FTAs concluded by China and ASEAN seem not to have been necessarily able to attain the 90% level. However, Japan and the EU are expected to make their best efforts to attain the highest tariff concession rate possible in their negotiations with these developing countries to level the playing field.

Impacts of the Japan-EU EPA on WTO Reform

The fact that the largest free advanced economic area of Japan and the EU, which share the common values of democracy, liberalism, and the rule of law, was created by concluding the Japan-EU EPA was a strong message for both parties to show their strong political will to raise the free trade flag high.[40] One of the main targets is to advance the WTO reform.

It is very well known that the Doha round, the latest round of trade negotiations among the WTO membership, which commenced in 2001, has stalled. The main reason the Doha round has stalled for the last twenty years is the conflict of interests, especially in agricultural sectors, between developed and developing countries.

The WTO reform is necessary not only to overcome the vulnerabilities of the WTO. Which has been unable to advance such multilateral talks as the Doha round to liberalize the world trade order, but also to improve conflict resolution mechanisms to prepare for the rapid pace of globalization and digitization. Furthermore, since the US President Donald Trump took office in 2017, the protectionism wave has been growing, and the tense trade conflicts between the US and China have continued.

To improve the situation, the EU presented a concept paper to modernise the WTO [11]. The concept paper consists of three parts:

1. Future EU proposals on rulemaking
2. Future EU proposals on regular work and transparency
3. Future EU proposals on dispute settlement.

The first part proposed[41]:

---

[39]TPP 11, which Japan concluded with 10 Asia–Pacific countries after the withdrawal of the US from the TPP in January 2017, came into effect in December, 2018, and the trade agreement between Japan and the US also came into effect in January 2020. Also, RCEP was signed in November 2020 by the 15 Asia-Pacific countries excluding India.

[40]Speech of PM Abe on July 26th, 2019 (https://www.kantei.go.jp/jp/97_abe/statement/2017/070 6kaiken.html).

[41]The main target seems to be China, although the paper does not mention its name.

I. For Future Rulemaking in the WTO

(A) to create rules that rebalance the system and level the playing field.
  – improve transparency and subsidy notifications,
  – better capture state-owned enterprises (SOEs), and.
  – more effectively capture the most trade-distortive types of subsidies.

(B) to establish new rules to address barriers to services and investment, including in the field of forced technology transfer:
  – need to address market access barriers, discriminatory treatment of foreign investors and behind the border distortions, including as they relate to forced technology transfer and other trade distortive policies, and.
  – need to address barriers to digital trade.

(C) to address the sustainability objectives of the global community:

II. For a new approach to flexibilities in the context of development objectives:
  – graduation,
  – special and differential treatment (SDT) in future agreements, and.
  – additional SDT in existing agreements.

III. To strengthen the procedural aspects of the WTO's rulemaking activities:
  – multilateral negotiations,
  – plurilateral negotiations, and.
  – role of the secretariat.

Ms. Cecilia Malmstrom, the former European Commissioner for Trade, expressed in November 2018 that the EU will support Japanese efforts to reform the WTO at the G20 meeting which was held in Osaka, Japan in 2019.[42] Thus, Japan and the EU are expected to play an indispensable role in the WTO reform.

4.5   Conclusions

The Japan-EU EPA was signed on 17 July 2018 after 18 negotiation rounds that started in April 2013, and finally became effective on 1 February 2019. As we have seen, the Japan-EU EPA was initiated by the Japanese industrial and business circle, because they were afraid of losing their competitiveness in the EU market after the EU-Korea FTA, which resulted in no duties on sensitive manufacturing products, took effect. Against the Japanese arguments, the EU industrial and business circle requested the elimination of NTBs in the Japanese market.

Almost one year has passed since the enforcement of the Japan-EU EPA, and the first-hand statistical data shows that it has produced positive results, as expected. As seen in Sect. 4.3, the Japan-EU EPA may expand its potential to upgrade other

---

[42] The Japantimes, 24th November, 2018 (https://www.japantimes.co.jp/news/2018/11/24/business/eu-trade-commissioner-expresses-supportjapans-goal-reform-wto/#.g8DA_xUuUl).

mega FTAs and facilitate WTO reform. Thus, the Japan-EU EPA is expected, first, to improve the bilateral economic relationship between Japan and the EU, and, second, to be a high-level bridge to facilitate economic partnerships around the globe.

However, there remain several concerns. The issue of most concern is Brexit. If the UK does not finish EPA/FTA negotiation during the transition period with, first, the EU and, second, Japan, by the end of 2020, renewed barriers might appear in trade with the UK.[43] Moreover, protectionist waves have not declined.

We must pay further attention to the implementation of the Japan-EU EPA and help it fulfil its potential.

References

1. Ando, M., & Kimura, F. (2013). Production Linkage of Asia and Europe via Central and Eastern Europe. *Journal of Economic Integration, 28–2*, 204–240.
2. Benz, S., & Yalcin, E. (2013). Quantifying the economic effects of an EU-Japan free trade agreement. Ludwig-Maximilians University's Center for Economic Studies and the Ifo Institute (CESIFO), *Working Papers*, No. 4319, 1–27.
3. Breinlich, H., Dhingra, S., & Ottaviano, G. (2016). How have EU's trade agreements impacted consumers? Centre for Economic Performance (CEP). *Discussion Paper*, No.1417, 1–49.
4. Cabinet Office. (2017). *Nichi-EU EPA tou no Keizai Kouka Bunseki* (in Japanese, *Analysis of Economic Impacts of Japan EU EPA and others*), Tokyo.
5. de Prado, C. (2014). Prospects for the EU-Japan strategic partnership: A global multi-level and swot analysis. *EU-Japan Centre for Industrial Cooperation* (pp. 1–68).
6. European Commission: EU Report. (2012). *Commission Staff Working Document: Impact Assessment Report on EU-Japan Trade Relations.*
7. European Commission: EU Report. (2015. *Trade Sustainability Impact Assessment of the Free Trade Agreement between the European Union and Japan: Interim Technical Report* (prepared by LSE Enterprise Ltd.).
8. European Commission: EU Report. (2016). *Annual Report on the Implementation on the Implementation of the EU-Korea Free Trade Agreement.*
9. European Commission. (2018). *The Economic Impact of the EU-Japan Economic Partnership Agreement (EPA): An analysis prepared by the European Commission's Directorate-General for Trade.*
10. European Parliament. (2018). *The EU-Japan Economic Partnership.*
11. European Union. (2018). *Concept Paper on WTO Modernisation.*
12. Felbermayr, G., Kimura, F., Okubo, T., & Steiningerd, M. (2019). Quantifying the EU-Japan economic partnership agreement. *Journal of the Japanese and International Economies, 51*, 110–128.
13. Japan External Trade Organization: JETRO. (2011). *EU Kankoku FTA no Gaiyou to Kaisetsu* (in Japanese, *Outline and Explanation of the FTA between the EU and Korea*).
14. JETRO. (2019). *Nichi-EU EPA Kaisetsusho* (in Japanese, *Handbook of Japan-EU EPA*).
15. Ministry of Agriculture, Agriculture and Fisheries: MAAF. (2016). *TPP ni okeru Juyo 5 Hinmoku-tou no Koushou Kekka* (in Japanese: *The TPP Negotiation Results of the 5 Important Items, etc.*). https://www.maff.go.jp/j/kokusai/tpp/pdf/2-1_5hinmoku_kekka.pdf.
16. Smeets, D. (2015). A free trade agreement between the EU and Japan—What is to be Expected? *Asia Europe Journal, 13*, 57–73.

---

[43]The EU and the U.K. agreed to conclude FTA on 25 December 2020, and EPA between Japan and the U.K. is to come into effect on 1 January 2021.

17. Sugita, S. (2006). Higashi Azaia wo Chushin-to-shita FTA/EPA Senryaku no Genjo Hyouka to Kadai (in Japanese: *Status Assessment and Tasks of FTA/EPA Strategies of East Asian Countries*), in Kansai Institute for Social and Economic Research: KISER, *Higashi Azaia Tougou Keizaiken to Kansai no Yakuwari ni-kansuru Kenkyu* (in Japanese, *A Research on East Asian Integrated Economic Area and the Role of Kansai Area*), https://www.apir.or.jp/wp/wp-content/uploads/82_01.pdf.

18. Sunesen, E. R., Francois, J. F., & Thelle, M. H. EU Report. (2009). *Assessment of Barriers to Trade and Investment between the EU and Japan, Copenhagen Economics.*

19. Toray Corporate Business Research, Inc. (2013). *Heisei 24-nendo Naigai Ittaika no Keizaiseicho-senryaku ni kakaru Kokusai-Keizai Chosa-Jigyo: Oshu Rengo tono Keizai-Renkei Sokushin no tameno Seido Bunseki Chosa* (in Japanese, *International Economic Research Project on the Economic Growth Agenda to Integrate Domestic and International Policies in the Fiscal Year 2013: An Institutional Analysis Survey to Promote the Economic Partnership with the European Union*).

20. Vicard, V. (2018), Une Estimation de l'Impact de Politiques Commerciales sur le PIB par les Noveaux Models Quantitatifs de Commerce, Counseil d'Analyse Economique Focus, No. 022-208.

21. Watanabe, Y. (2013). Japan-EU EPA: Short history and prospects of the new Japan-EU cooperation" (in Japanese), in Japan institution of international affairs. *International Affairs,* No.632, 29–39.

22. Yamashita, K. (2016). *Bata ga Kaenai Futsugou na Shinjitsu* (in Japanese: *An inconvenient truth that we cannot buy Butter*), Gentousha (pp. 1–145).

23. Yoshii, M. (2014). Nihon-EU Kankei no Shorai, (in Japanese, The Future of Relationships between Japan and the EU). In M. Yoshii, & M. Kubo (Eds.), *EU Togo no Shinka to Euro Kiki – Kakudai*, (in Japanese, *Deepening and Enlargement of the EU Integration, and the Euro Crisis)*, Keiso Shobo, xiv+194.

24. Yoshii, M. (2016). Nichi-EU Kosho no Ronten: EU-Kankoku FTA no Keiken kara (in Japanese, Japan-EU EPA Negotiation: Lessons from EU-South Korea FTA. *Kokumin-Keizai-Zasshi, 213*(3), 15–30.

Chapter 5
The Effects of Brexit on Prices Under the EU–Japan EPA

Taiji Hagiwara

Abstract The EU–Japan Economic Partnership Agreement (EPA) came into force in February 2019. However, the United Kingdom left the European Union in January 2020, and is currently negotiating new tariff regimes (as in February 2020). If negotiations fail, trade tariffs from the Most Favourable Nations (MFN) agreement will be imposed between the United Kingdom and European Union. In addition, every free trade agreement (FTA) that the United Kingdom agreed through the European Union, including the EU–Japan EPA, will need to be renegotiated. We investigate the effects of the withdrawal of the United Kingdom from the European Union, colloquially known as Brexit, on prices under the EU–Japan EPA. The EPA allowed reduced tariffs between Japan and EU-28 countries. Failed negotiations will increase the tariff rates between EU-27 countries and the United Kingdom. We analyse the change in prices of traded goods and services by sector using an inter-country input-output table compiled by the OECD.

Keywords EU-japan economic partnership agreement · Tariff reduction · Brexit · Inter-country input-output table

5.1 Introduction

The EU–Japan Economic Partnership Agreement (EPA) came into force in February 2019. However, the United Kingdom left the European Union in January 2020, and is currently negotiating new tariff regimes (as in February 2020). If negotiations fail, trade tariffs from the Most Favourable Nations (MFN) agreement will be imposed between the United Kingdom and European Union. In addition, every free trade agreement (FTA) that the United Kingdom agreed through the European Union, including the EU–Japan EPA, will need to be renegotiated.

T. Hagiwara (✉)
Graduate School of Economics, Kobe University, 2-1 Rokkodai-cho,
Nada, Kobe 657-8501, Japan
e-mail: hagiwara@econ.kobe-u.ac.jp

© Kobe University 2021   75
M. Yoshii and C.-D. Yi (eds.), *An Economic Analysis of Korea–EU FTA and Japan–EU EPA*, Kobe University Monograph Series in Social Science Research,
https://doi.org/10.1007/978-981-33-6145-4_5

We investigate the effects of the withdrawal of the United Kingdom from the European Union, colloquially known as Brexit, on prices under the EU–Japan EPA. The EPA allowed reduced tariffs between Japan and EU-28 countries. Failed negotiations will increase the tariff rates between EU-27 countries and the United Kingdom. Although the change in tariff rates and, by extension, prices will affect trade directions, we do not analyse this circular effect because of the ambiguity in the price elasticity of imports of similar products produced in different countries (the Armington elasticity). We simply analyse the change in prices of traded goods and services by sector using an inter-country input-output table compiled by the OECD. We assume fixed input coefficients, including the import coefficients. Therefore, we assume the change in prices will be greater, and the change in outputs smaller (close to zero), than when an import substitution policy is implemented.

5.2 Model

The inter-country input-output (ICIO) table contains r countries and n sectors in each country. Each sector inputs goods and services from various countries proportionate to its output level. That is, the unit production of the sector j in country s requires a_{ij}^{rs} units of commodity i made by the sector in country r. The input coefficient a_{ij}^{rs} is constant and independent from change in the relative price. Country s levies tariffs on commodity i imported from country r at an *ad valorem* tariff rate:

$$t_i^{rs} \begin{cases} \geq 0, r \neq s \\ = 0, r = s \end{cases}.$$

Furthermore, the labour input coefficient l_j^s, nominal wage rate w^s, and profit per output π_j^s are constant. The latter two are measured by a common currency, the US Dollar. Thus, the value-added coefficient $v_j^s = w^s l_j^s + \pi_j^s$ is constant. The prices of sector j in country s are:

$$p_j^s = v_j^s + \sum_r \sum_i p_i^r \left(1 + t_i^{rs}\right) a_{ij}^{rs}$$

The price equation can be rewritten in matrix form:

$$p = v + pA$$

where

$$p \equiv \left(\begin{matrix} p_1^1 & \cdots & p_N^1 & \cdots & p_1^R & \cdots & p_N^R \end{matrix} \right)$$

$$v \equiv \left(\begin{matrix} v_1^1 & \cdots & v_N^1 & \cdots & v_1^R & \cdots & v_N^R \end{matrix} \right)$$

$$A = \begin{pmatrix} a_{11}^{11} & \cdots & a_{1N}^{11} & (1+t_1^{1R})a_{11}^{1R} & \cdots & (1+t_1^{1R})a_{1N}^{1R} \\ \vdots & \ddots & \vdots & \cdots & \vdots & \ddots & \vdots \\ a_{N1}^{11} & \cdots & a_{NN}^{11} & (1+t_N^{1R})a_{N1}^{1R} & \cdots & (1+t_N^{1R})a_{NN}^{1R} \\ \vdots & & \vdots & \ddots & & \vdots \\ (1+t_1^{R1})a_{11}^{R1} & \cdots & (1+t_1^{R1})a_{1N}^{R1} & a_{11}^{RR} & \cdots & a_{1N}^{RR} \\ \vdots & \ddots & \vdots & \cdots & \vdots & \ddots & \vdots \\ (1+t_N^{R1})a_{N1}^{R1} & \cdots & (1+t_N^{R1})a_{NN}^{R1} & a_{N1}^{RR} & \cdots & a_{NN}^{RR} \end{pmatrix}$$

Matrix A represents the multiplication of input coefficients a_{ij}^{rs} and tariff rates t_i^{rs}. Since tariffs are not levied on domestic inputs, $t_i^{ss}=0$, and the coefficients for own country are simply the input coefficient a_{ij}^{ss}.

If a country changes a tariff rate $t_i^{rs'}$ with fixed input coefficient a_{ij}^{rs} and value added coefficient v_j^s, the new prices $p_j^{s'}$ will be:

$$p_j^{s'} = v_j^s + \sum_r \sum_i p_i^{r'} \left(1 + t_i^{rs'}\right) a_{ij}^{rs}$$

Taking the difference:

$$p_j^{s'} - p_j^s = \sum_r \sum_i \left(p_i^{r'} - p_i^r\right)\left(1 + t_i^{rs'}\right)a_{ij}^{rs} + \sum_r \sum_i p_i^r \left(t_i^{rs'} - t_i^{rs}\right)a_{ij}^{rs}$$

$$\Delta p_j^s = \sum_r \sum_i \Delta p_i^r \left(1 + t_i^{rs'}\right)a_{ij}^{rs} + \sum_r \sum_i p_i^r \Delta t_i^{rs} a_{ij}^{rs}$$

$$\Delta p_j^s = \sum_r \sum_i \left(p_i^r \Delta t_i^{rs} a_{ij}^{rs}\right)b_{ij}^{rs}$$

where b_{ij}^{rs} is $((r-1)N+i, (s-1)N+j)$ is the factor of the Leontief inverse matrix:

$$p' = v + p'A$$

$$p' - p = (p' - p)A + p'(A' - A)$$

$$\Delta p = \Delta p + p'\Delta A = p'\Delta A(I - A)^{-1} = p'\Delta AB \cong p\Delta AB$$

Tariff rate changes are reflected in the change in A.

5.3 Data

The main data used are: (1) the ICIO table; (2) the tariff rates of the current MFN and the tariff reduction schedule of the EU–Japan EPA; and (3) the import data, as shown below.

We use the ICIO table from the 2018 edition[1] compiled by OECD. It contains 65 countries, including EU-28 countries and Japan, and 36 sectors. The detailed sector list is shown in the Appendix Table.

MFN rates can be obtained from the WTO homepage[2]; they were downloaded by HS code at the 6-digit level. The tariff reduction schedule of the EU–Japan EPA is from Annex 2-A, 'Tariff elimination and reduction', of the EU–Japan EPA.[3] In Japan, 9-digit codes are used to classify commodities, and represent approximately 7,200 items. In the European Union, 8-digit codes can be used to classify commodities.

Tariff rates were aggregated against the classifications in the OECD ICIO table, and weighted by the amount of the import.[4] Although EU countries forming customs union and tariff rates at detailed levels are common, the aggregated tariff rates imposed by EU countries on Japan, and the tariff rate imposed by Japan on EU countries, are different between EU countries because of the different weights. The calculated tariff rates are shown in Table 5.1. Columns X and Z represent the average weights by output and intermediate input, respectively.

Among the EU tariff rates imposed on Japanese products, the highest MFN rate was for 05 Food, Beverage and Tobacco (9%), followed by 06 Textiles and 18 Motor Vehicle (7%), then 11 Rubber and Plastics and 19 Other Transport Equipment (4%). The tariff rates for 07 Wood and 17 Machinery in column Z are higher than those in column X, which means that these sectors are used to produce intermediate products rather than final products. After the EPA came into force in 2019, almost all tariffs were reduced to zero. Although tariffs in several sectors remain positive, though less than 1%, they are expected to reduce to zero by 2036.

In the case of Japan's tariff rates imposed on EU products, the highest MFN rate was 05 Food, Beverage and Tobacco (36% in weighted output, and 40% in intermediated input). The second highest MFN rate was 06 Textiles and Apparels (10%). Under the EPA, 06 Textiles and Apparel (4%), 05 Food, Beverage and Tobacco (3%), 07 Wood (3%) and 01 Agriculture (2%) remain positive. Though, they are expected to diminish.

---

[1]Data is downloadable from OECD. https://www.oecd.org/sti/ind/inter-country-input-output-tables.htm.

[2]https://data.wto.org. MFN by detailed HS code in 'Tariff indicators—Applied'.

[3]EU-Japan Economic Partnership Agreement. https://trade.ec.europa.eu/doclib/press/index.cfm?id=1684.

[4]For Japanese import, Trade Statistics Data for Japan (https://www.e-stat.go.jp). For EU import data, Comext in Eurostat (https://ec.europa.eu/eurostat). Aggregation is based on Bilateral Trade in Goods by Industry and End-use Category (https://oe.cd/btd) and OECD ICIO Tables (https:oe.cd/icio).

Table 5.1 Tariff rates

Sector	EU tariff on Japanese products				Japan's tariff on EU products			
	MFN 2017		EPA 2019		MFN 2017		EPA 2019	
	X (%)	Z (%)	X (%)	Z (%)	X (%)	Z (%)	X (%)	Z (%)
01 Agriculture	1.64	1.61	0.00	0.00	4.92	4.96	2.65	2.77
02 Mining energy	0.00	0.00	0.00	0.00	0.00	0.00	0.00	0.00
03 Mining non-energy	0.31	0.32	0.00	0.00	0.00	0.00	0.00	0.00
04 Mining services	0.00	0.00	0.00	0.00	0.00	0.00	0.00	0.00
05 Food, beverages	9.26	9.19	0.06	0.06	36.62	40.08	3.71	3.88
06 Textiles, apparel	7.43	7.29	0.00	0.00	10.11	10.03	4.38	4.36
07 Wood	1.31	1.37	0.00	0.00	3.07	3.18	3.07	3.18
08 Paper and printing	0.05	0.05	0.00	0.00	0.01	0.01	0.00	0.00
09 Coke and petroleum	0.21	0.26	0.00	0.00	0.15	0.19	0.00	0.00
10 Chemicals	2.84	2.83	0.03	0.03	0.66	0.72	0.02	0.03
11 Rubber and plastic	4.71	4.70	0.07	0.07	2.21	2.19	0.00	0.00
12 Other non-metals	2.87	2.86	0.01	0.01	1.38	1.39	0.17	0.16
13 Basic metals	0.88	0.87	0.03	0.03	1.11	1.10	0.00	0.00
14 Fabricated metals	3.00	3.00	0.02	0.02	1.04	1.01	0.00	0.00
15 Computer, electronics	1.10	1.09	0.03	0.03	0.00	0.00	0.00	0.00
16 Electric equipment	2.46	2.44	0.01	0.01	0.03	0.03	0.00	0.00
17 Machinery	1.63	1.71	0.03	0.04	0.00	0.00	0.00	0.00
18 Motor vehicles	7.11	6.94	0.55	0.51	0.00	0.00	0.00	0.00
19 Other transport equipment	4.36	4.33	0.31	0.30	0.00	0.00	0.00	0.00
20 Other manufacturing	1.58	1.55	0.00	0.00	1.44	1.39	0.08	0.07

Note X represents the average tariff weighted by output, and Z represents the average tariff weighted by intermediate input

5.4 Simulation Results

Instead of simply listing headings of different levels we recommend to let every heading be followed by at least a short passage of text. Further on please use the LATEX automatism for all your cross-references and citations as has already been described in Sect. 2.

5.4.1 Scenario 1: EU–Japan EPA

The results of the EU–Japan EPA is shown in Table 5.2. In all sectors in the European Union and Japan, prices decrease. Since the absolute magnitude of the changes is small, we focus on relative magnitude. In the European Union, 18 Motor Vehicles showed the largest decrease in price (−0.034% in 2019 and -0.036% in 2036). The greatest decrease in prices was observed in Belgium (−0.212%), Estonia (-0.159%), Cyprus (-0.137%), and Malta (−0.097%). Apart from Belgium (which has an estimated production value of 16 billion US$), these countries have relatively small Motor Vehicle production. Among the largest countries in Motor Vehicle production are Germany (424 billion US$, −0.026%), the United Kingdom (80 billion US$, -0.028%), Spain (71 billion US$, −0.057%), Italy (65 billion US$, -0.028%), and France (60 billion US$, -0.032%). Spain clearly has the largest production value. Eastern European countries declined on average (−0.034%): Hungary by −0.040%, Slovakia by −0.037%, Czech by −0.036%, and Poland by −0.029%.

In Japan, the sectors with the greatest price decreases are 25 Accommodation and Food Services (−0.083%), 05 Food Products, Beverages and Tobacco (−0.070%), 01 Agriculture, Forestry and Fishing (-0.056%), and 06 Textiles, Wearing Apparel, Leather and Related Products (−0.047%). The price decrease in 25 Accommodation and Food Services was caused by a tariff reduction in 05 Food Products, Beverages and Tobacco.

Because of the gradual reduction of tariffs, prices are expected to gradually decrease until 2036. However, few changes are expected between 2019 and 2036 in the European Union. The greatest reductions were in 18 Motor Vehicles and 19 Other Transport Equipment, by 0.002% and 0.001%, respectively. On the other hand, almost all sectors in Japan experienced a decrease in their prices by more than 0.001%. The largest decreasing sector is 06 Textiles (0.030%), followed by 07 Wood and Wood Products (0.020%).

5.4.2 Scenario 2: EU–Japan EPA but hard Brexit with EU-27

Next, we consider what happens if the United Kingdom fails to agree new FTAs with EU-27 (i.e. hard Brexit) and Japan. Although the United Kingdom is renegotiating

Table 5.2 Price changes under the EU–Japan EPA

Sector	EU28		Japan	
	2019 (%)	2036 (%)	2019 (%)	2036 (%)
01 Agriculture	0.00	0.00	−0.06	−0.06
02 Mining energy	0.00	0.00	−0.01	−0.01
03 Mining non-energy	0.00	0.00	−0.01	−0.01
04 Mining services	0.00	0.00	−0.01	−0.01
05 Food, beverages	0.00	0.00	−0.07	−0.08
06 Textiles, apparel	−0.01	−0.01	−0.05	−0.08
07 Wood	0.00	0.00	−0.02	−0.04
08 Paper and printing	0.00	0.00	−0.01	−0.02
09 Coke and petroleum	0.00	0.00	−0.01	−0.01
10 Chemicals	−0.01	−0.01	−0.03	−0.03
11 Rubber and plastic	−0.01	−0.01	−0.02	−0.03
12 Other non-metals	-0.01	−0.01	−0.01	−0.01
13 Basic metals	−0.01	−0.01	−0.01	−0.01
14 Fabricated metals	−0.01	−0.01	−0.01	−0.01
15 Computer, electronics	−0.01	−0.01	−0.01	−0.01
16 Electric equipment	−0.01	−0.01	−0.01	−0.01
17 Machinery	−0.01	−0.01	−0.01	−0.01
18 Motor vehicles	−0.03	−0.04	−0.01	−0.01
19 Other transport equipment	−0.02	−0.02	−0.01	−0.02
20 Other manufacturing	−0.01	−0.01	−0.02	−0.03
21 Electricity, gas	0.00	0.00	−0.01	−0.01
22 Construction	0.00	0.00	−0.01	−0.01
23 Wholesale & retail	0.00	0.00	−0.01	−0.01
24 Transportation	0.00	0.00	−0.01	−0.01
25 Accommodation	0.00	0.00	−0.08	−0.10
26 Publishing	0.00	0.00	−0.01	−0.01
27 Telecommunications	0.00	0.00	0.00	−0.01
28 IT & IT services	0.00	0.00	0.00	−0.01
29 Finance and insurance	0.00	0.00	0.00	−0.01
30 Real estate	0.00	0.00	0.00	0.00
31 Other business services	0.00	0.00	−0.01	−0.01
32 Public administration	0.00	0.00	−0.01	−0.01
33 Education	0.00	0.00	−0.01	−0.01
34 Health and social works	0.00	0.00	−0.02	−0.02
35 Entertainment	0.00	0.00	−0.01	−0.02
36 Private household	0.00	0.00	0.00	0.00

Table 5.3 Price changes under hard brexit

Sector	EU27	UK	Japan
	2021 (%)	2021 (%)	2021 (%)
01 Agriculture	0.04	0.57	−0.06
02 Mining energy	0.01	0.08	−0.01
03 Mining non-energy	0.01	0.14	−0.01
04 Mining services	0.01	0.11	−0.01
05 Food, beverages	0.07	0.88	−0.07
06 Textiles, apparel	0.03	0.30	−0.05
07 Wood	0.02	0.40	−0.02
08 Paper and printing	0.02	0.16	−0.01
09 Coke and petroleum	0.01	0.07	−0.01
10 Chemicals	0.04	0.30	−0.03
11 Rubber and plastic	0.04	0.33	−0.02
12 Other non-metals	0.02	0.20	−0.01
13 Basic metals	0.02	0.23	−0.01
14 Fabricated metals	0.02	0.19	−0.01
15 Computer, electronics	0.02	0.21	−0.01
16 Electric equipment	0.02	0.30	−0.01
17 Machinery	0.02	0.28	−0.01
18 Motor vehicles	0.05	0.78	−0.01
19 Other transport equipment	0.05	0.34	−0.01
20 Other manufacturing	0.02	0.18	−0.02
21 Electricity, gas	0.01	0.07	−0.01
22 Construction	0.02	0.16	−0.01
23 Wholesale & retail	0.01	0.15	−0.01
24 Transportation	0.01	0.11	0.00
25 Accommodation	0.04	0.56	−0.09
26 Publishing	0.01	0.06 ara>	−0.01
27 Telecommunications	0.01	0.11	0.00
28 IT & IT services	0.01	0.06	0.00
29 Finance and insurance	0.01	0.06	0.00
30 Real estate	0.00	0.02	0.00
31 Other business services	0.01	0.08	−0.01
32 Public administration	0.01	0.11	−0.01
33 Education	0.00	0.05	−0.01
34 Health and social works	0.01	0.10	−0.02
35 Entertainment	0.01	0.11	−0.01
36 Private household	0.00	0.00	0.00

international agreements that were made when it was a member of the European Union, it may not have a trade agreement with EU-27 and Japan. If this were to happen, the MFN tariff rates will be imposed on trade between the United Kingdom, and EU-27 and Japan. Thus, 2017 MFN tariff rates were imposed on UK trade with EU-27 and Japan, while the 2021 EPA tariff rates were imposed on trade between EU-27 and Japan. The results are shown in Table 5.3.

The prices in both EU-27 and the United Kingdom increase, while the prices in Japan decrease. The magnitude of the price increases in the United Kingdom is larger than those in EU-27. The highest increase was observed in 05 Food (0.879% in the United Kingdom, 0.067% in EU-27), followed by 18 Motor Vehicle (0.782% in the United Kingdom, 0.050% in EU-27), 01 Agriculture (0.782% in the United Kingdom, 0.050% in EU-27), and 25 Accommodation and Food Services (0.557% in the United Kingdom, 0.037% in EU-27).

5.5 Conclusion

In this chapter, we evaluate the price effects of the EU–Japan EPA and Brexit. Although the magnitude of the decrease in prices is small, EU-27 and Japan enjoy cost reductions. However, if renegotiations for a new FTA between the United Kingdom and EU-27 fail, costs will increase and international competitiveness of the United Kingdom will be low.

5.6 Appendix: Sector List

Sector	Description
01 Agriculture	Agriculture, forestry and fishing
02 Mining energy	Mining and extraction of energy producing products
03 Mining non-energy	Mining and quarrying of non-energy producing products
04 Mining services	Mining support service activities
05 Food, beverages	Food products, beverages and tobacco
06 Textiles, apparel	Textiles, wearing apparel, leather and related products
07 Wood	Wood and products of wood and cork
08 Paper and printing	Paper products and printing
09 Coke and petroleum	Coke and refined petroleum products
10 Chemicals	Chemicals and pharmaceutical products
11 Rubber and plastic	Rubber and plastic products
12 Other non-metals	Other non-metallic mineral products

(continued)

(continued)

Sector	Description
13 Basic metals	Basic metals
14 Fabricated metals	Fabricated metal products
15 Computer, electronics	Computer, electronic and optical products
16 Electric equipment	Electrical equipment
17 Machinery	Machinery and equipment, nec
18 Motor vehicles	Motor vehicles, trailers and semi-trailers
19 Other transport equipment	Other transport equipment
20 Other manufacturing	Other manufacturing; repair and installation of machinery and equipment
21 Electricity, gas	Electricity, gas, water supply, sewerage, waste and remediation services
22 Construction	Construction
23 Wholesale & retail	Wholesale and retail trade; repair of motor vehicles
24 Transportation	Transportation and storage
25 Accommodation	Accommodation and food services
26 Publishing	Publishing, audiovisual and broadcasting activities
27 Telecommunications	Telecommunications
28 IT & IT services	IT and other information services
29 Finance and insurance	Financial and insurance activities
30 Real estate	Real estate activities
31 Other business services	Other business sector services
32 Public administration	Public admin. and defense; compulsory social security
33 Education	Education
34 Health and social works	Human health and social work
35 Entertainment	Arts, entertainment, recreation and other service activities
36 Private household	Private households with employed persons

Chapter 6
Expectations of Japanese Small and Medium Enterprises Regarding the EU–Japan Economic Partnership Agreement. Analysis from an Independent Survey

Massimiliano Porto

Abstract We investigate the expectations of Japanese small and medium enterprises (SMEs) regarding the effects of the EU–Japan Economic Partnership Agreement (EPA) on their exports to the European Union through an analysis of their responses to an independent survey. The survey targets Japanese exporting SMEs, including those that currently do not export to the European Union. We built the database of Japanese exporting SMEs based on information available from the Japan External Trade Organization, business association websites, local trade directories, and so on. The survey contains 26 questions structured in three parts. The questions aim to identify the profile of the respondent firms in the first part, their approach to the European Union's markets in the second part, and the opinion of the Japanese exporting SMEs on the EU–Japan EPA in the third part. From the responses to the survey, it can be seen that even though most respondents do not think that the EU–Japan EPA will help increase their exports to EU markets, most of them would have preferred an earlier implementation. This could imply firms' preference for an easier export framework, which is favoured by the application of EPAs.

Keywords Eu–japan economic partnership agreement · Small and medium enterprises · Internationalization

6.1 Introduction

Small and Medium Enterprises (SMEs) represent the backbone of any domestic economy because of their important role in the socio-economic development of the country with their contribution to employment and innovation. Compared with

M. Porto (✉)
Kobe University, 2-1 Rokkodai-cho, Nada-ku, Kobe 657-8501, Japan
e-mail: massimiliano.porto@people.kobe-u.ac.jp

© Kobe University 2021

M. Yoshii and C.-D. Yi (eds.), *An Economic Analysis of Korea–EU FTA and Japan–EU EPA*, Kobe University Monograph Series in Social Science Research, https://doi.org/10.1007/978-981-33-6145-4_6

Table 6.1 Definition of Japanese SME

Industry	SMEs (meet one or more of the following conditions)		Small enterprises included among SMEs at left
	Capital	No. of regular employees	No. of regular employees
(1) Manufacturing and others	Up to ¥300 million	Up to 300	Up to 20
(2) Wholesale	Up to ¥100 million	Up to 100	Up to 5
(3) Services	Up to ¥50 million	Up to 100	Up to 5
(4) Retail	Up to ¥50 million	Up to 50	Up to 5

large firms and multinationals, SMEs are more fragile due to constraints such as financial resources and human capital, which make harder to survive, especially during economic crisis. For this reason, national governments launch programs and policies to support SMEs.

In Japan, the scopes and definition of SMEs are stated under Article 2 of the Small and Medium-sized Enterprise Basic Act [4]. A Japanese firm is classified as SME if it meets conditions based on capital and number of regular employees. These criteria depend on the industry (Table 6.1).[1]

Japanese SMEs account for about 99.7% of all Japanese enterprises and contribute to 70% of all jobs in Japan. They are engaged in different business sectors and therefore cannot be considered a homogeneous group. However, the median values from the Credit Risk Database (CRD) show that a typical SME has three employees, sales of ¥67.9 million, ordinary profits of ¥1.6 million, total assets of ¥54.2 million, and capital of ¥5.1 million. As such, the Ministry of Economy Trade and Industry (METI) concludes that the typical SME in Japan is rather small [5, p. 29].

According to METI, the number of Japanese exporting SMEs grew from 3,445 in 2001 to 4,544 in 2015. Furthermore, in the same period, the ratio of exporting companies increased from 17 to 21%. The export value and export-to-sales ratio of SMEs increased as well. The export value increased from ¥2.6 trillion in 2001 to ¥6.2 trillion in 2015 while the export-to-sales ratio rose from 2.3% in 2001 to 4.1% in 2015. Furthermore, METI reports that internationalized SMEs are more productive. In particular, labour productivity is higher among enterprises that have achieved overseas expansion than those that have not, and it is also higher among enterprises that engage in exports than those that do not [5, pp. 24–25].[2]

---

[1]Refer to The Small and Medium Enterprise Agency (SMEA) of the Ministry of Economy Trade and Industry (METI) ([5]: xi) for more details regarding the classification of Japanese SMEs.

[2]METI considers as overseas expansion enterprises those enterprises which have at least one subsidiary or affiliate overseas.

Japan provides different programs to support the overseas expansion of SMEs such as the "Program for supporting overseas expansion by SMEs and micro businesses" whose budget for 2018 was ¥2.04 billion and the "JAPAN Brand Development Assistance Program" whose budget for 2018 was ¥1.05 billion. The "Program for supporting overseas expansion by SMEs and micro businesses" provides strategic support such as information on overseas market trends and regulations, implementation of feasibility studies, and the establishment of an export framework, as well as support for participating in trade fairs in Japan and overseas and so on. The "JAPAN Brand Development Assistance Program" provides support such as for the formulation of strategies built on collaboration among multiple SMEs, product development based on those strategies and participation in overseas trade fairs [5, p. 416].

In this context, Economic Partnership Agreements (EPAs) (or Free Trade Agreements (FTAs)) can be considered an indirect policy to support the overseas expansion of firms.[3] In fact, contrary to the above-mentioned programs, EPAs indirectly support the overseas expansion of enterprises by eliminating import tariffs and reducing the negative impact of non-tariff measures (NTMs) to facilitate access to the partner's market.

The position of enterprises in Japan in relation to EPAs can be summarized by the statements of the Japanese Business Federation (Nippon Keidanren), which demanded that the Japanese government take a more active external economic policy [1, 2]. Referring to the access of Japanese firms to European Union (EU) markets, the chairman of the Keidanren, Hiromasa Yonekura, wrote in 2012 to European political and business leaders, calling for negotiations on an EU–Japan EPA to start as soon as possible [3]. The negotiations between Japan and the EU were officially launched in March 2013. After 18 rounds, the negotiations for the EPA were finalized on 8 December 2017. On 17 July 2018, the EU and Japan signed the agreement in Tokyo. Finally, on 1 February 2019 the EU–Japan EPA came into force.

In this study, we are interested in analysing the expectations of the Japanese SMEs regarding the effects of the EU–Japan EPA on their exports to the EU and whether they preferred an earlier implementation of the agreement.

6.2 Survey Structure

The survey was administered to Japanese exporting SMEs between 1 November 2018 and 7 January 2019 over email. The contacts database for Japanese SMEs was built from multiple sources: the Japan External Trade Organization (JETRO); Ministry of Agriculture, Forestry and Fisheries (MAFF); Prefecture Trade Directory; business associations; and firms' websites.

---

[3]Basically, EPAs are broader agreements that include the contents of FTAs. However, given that many of the FTAs that have been recently signed are comprehensive agreements more than simple tariff elimination agreements, the distinction between FTA and EPA is not neat. In this paper, we use the terms FTA and EPA interchangeably.

The survey is made up of 26 questions organized into three sections: firm profile, approach to the EU markets, and access to the EU markets.

6.2.1 Firm Profile

The firm profile section of the survey consists of 13 questions. The following questions aim at identifying the profile of the respondent firm, such as company size, structure, and internationalization:

1.1   location of the headquarters.
1.2   number of regular employees.
1.3   amount of capital.
1.4   type of business entity.
1.5   whether the firm is part of a group.
1.6   number of business years.
1.7   business sector.
1.8   whether the products are processed only in Japan or overseas as well.
1.9   number of exporting years.
1.10 number of exporting markets.
1.11 degree of internationalization, formulated as the ratio between revenue from exports over total revenue.
1.12 approach to foreign markets.
1.13 whether the firm already has experience with other EPAs signed by Japan.

6.2.2 Approach to the EU Markets

This section of the survey consists of seven questions. The following questions aim at identifying Japanese SMEs' approach to the EU markets and the degree of their internationalization activities in EU markets:

2.1   asks the respondent firm to assess different world geographical markets such as the EU, USA, China, and so on. This question aims at comparing the interest of the respondent firm in world markets.
2.2   number of exporting years to the EU.
2.3   number of exporting markets to the EU.
2.4   importance of the EU markets for the Japanese SME, formulated as total revenue from the EU market over total exports.
2.5   approach to the EU markets.

We added two questions for the firms that, in response to question 2.5, indicated that they have set up a firm in the EU:

2.6   how the firm established the business entity in the EU.
2.7   share of the capital in the established firm in the EU.

6.2.3 *Access to EU Markets*

The access to the EU markets section of the survey consists of six questions. The following questions aim at identifying the opinions of the Japanese SMEs about access to the EU markets and the EU–Japan EPA:

3.1 overall assessment of the access to the EU markets.

3.2 assessment regarding the main barriers to trade, such as tariff barrier, technical barriers, conformity assessment, certificate of origin, and so on.

3.3 whether the respondent firm thinks that the EU–Japan EPA will contribute to increasing its exports to the EU markets.

3.4 whether the respondent firm preferred an earlier implementation of the EU–Japan EPA.

3.5 whether the implementation of the EU–Japan EPA will contribute to modifying its strategy towards the EU markets.

3.6 whether the EU–South Korea FTA gave an advantage to Korean competitors in the EU markets.

Finally, we asked the details of the respondent to the survey such as name, employment position, telephone number and email address.

6.3 Analysis of the Responses

In total, we submitted the survey by email to 1984 firms. We received 107 responses from Japanese SMEs from 24 Japanese prefectures: 13 firms each from Ehime and Gifu, 12 firms from Osaka, 8 firms Iwate, 7 firms each from Miyagi and Tokyo, 6 firms each from Kagawa and Fukui, 5 firms each from Akita and Mie, 3 firms each from Fukushima, Aichi, Kanagawa and Tokushima, 2 firms each from Hiroshima, Toyama and Ishikawa, and 1 firm each from Chiba, Shizuoka, Kochi, Yamagata, Okayama, Kyoto, and Ibaraki. Figure 6.1 shows the distribution of the respondent firms by prefecture.

However, 25 firms partially answered the survey questions while three firms, even though they submitted the completed surveys, were not SMEs. Therefore, these firms have been excluded from the following analysis. The final sample is made up of 79 firms that answered all the questions of the survey and are classified as SMEs.

In terms of designation, 55 out of 79 respondents identified themselves as president or CEO of the respondent firms (*shachō, kaichō, daihyō torishimariyaku, jōmu torishimariyaku*), one as vice-president (*fuku shachō*), and the remaining 23 as manager (*eria manējā, kaigai jigyō buchō, kanri hon buchō, kikaku-shitsu shitsuchō, and so on*).

There are 35 small enterprises in the sample (seven firms have 1–5 employees, thirteen firms have 6–10 employees, and fifteen firms have 11–20 employees). The remaining 44 firms have the following number of employees: twenty firms have

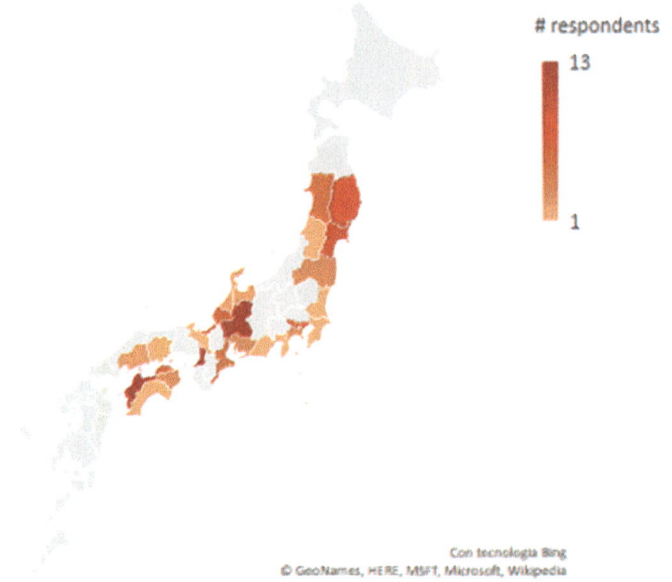

Fig. 6.1 Distribution of respondent firms by prefecture

21–50 employees, twelve firms have 51–100 employees, ten firms have 101–300 employees, and two firms have more than 300 employees.

Most of the firms have capital up to ¥50 million (60 firms) while 16 firms have capital up to ¥100 million and only three firms have capital more than ¥300 million. Most of the firms (71) are limited companies (Ltd.) (*kabushikigaisha*), two firms are limited liability companies (LLC) (*gōdōkaisha*), and six firms answered that they belong to an "other" business entity categorization. Most firms in the sample (72) are independent, while seven firms are parts of groups. Business lifespans include 63 firms which have been in business for more than 30 years, six firms between 11 and 15 years, five firms between 6 and 10 years, three firms between 16 and 20 years, one firm between 21 and 25 years and one firm between 1 and 5 years.

Most of the firms belong to two sectors: Food & Beverage (29) and Machinery (15). Four firms each belong to Electronics, Metal Products, and Services; three firms to the Wood sector; two firms to Ceramics; and one firm each to Furniture, Medical Products, Optical Parts, Raw Material, and Transportation Equipment. Thirteen firms answered they belong to a different sector ("Other"). Most of the firms (58) answered that their products are processed only in Japan; 13 firms answered that they are processed in particular in Japan; six firms that they are processed particularly abroad, and two firms answered that their products are processed 50–50 between Japan and overseas.

By focusing on the international activities of the sample firms, we find out that 18 firms have been exporting for 1–5 years, 12 firms for 6–10 years, 11 firms for 11–15 years, nine firms for 16–20 years, five firms for 21–25 years, six firms for 26–30 years, and 18 firms for more than 30 years. Export geographical diversity varies: 32 firms in the sample export to 1–5 markets, 19 firms to 6–10 markets, 16 firms export to 15–20 markets, and 12 firms export to more than 25 markets. In addition, 28 out of the 79 firms of the sample do not export to the EU markets. 51 firms answered that the ratio between revenue from exports over total revenue is less than 10%, 17 firms answered that it is between 10 and 25%, seven firms between 25 and 50%, and only four firms answered that their revenues from exports account for a ratio between 50 and 75%. If we consider the degree of internationalization based on whether firms export to the EU or they do not, we find that the revenues from export account for less than 10 for 82.1% of the firms that do not export to the EU and for 54.9% of the firms that export to the EU. However, if we consider the total number of respondent firms whose degree of internationalization is less than 25%, it results that they are 92.8% of the firms that do not export to the EU and 82.3% of the firms that export to the EU. This confirms the low degree of internationalization of the firms of the sample, regardless of exports to the EU.

Figure 6.2 shows this information regarding the internationalization of the firms in the sample by exporting years, business sector, and by whether they export to EU markets. Within the two more represented sectors of our sample, Food & Beverage and Machinery, most of the firms in Food & Beverage have been exporting for up to 20 years while most of the firms in Machinery have been doing so for more than 20 years. In addition, most of the firms that export to the EU markets export to a larger number of markets.

Most of the firms in the sample approach international markets through direct sales (59) and agents (47). Only seven firms approach international markets through overseas establishments as well (six set up branches and three set up overseas plants as well). Fourteen firms also answered they use an "other" approach for international markets.

The survey shows that only nine firms in the sample (11.4%) have experience with other EPAs signed by Japan. Three firms specified that they use the EPA signed by Japan with Thailand. With regard to the Japan-Thailand EPA, one respondent assessed it very positively because "duties are not due and because it makes easier to export" (*kanzei ga kakaranaku naru no wa, yushutsu shi yasuku nari yoi seido da to omoimasu*).

The next responses explain the interest and approach of respondent firms to the EU markets. Figure 6.3 shows the interest of the respondent firms in the world markets, where 0 means "not interested" and 5 "very interested". The region "Asia (excluding China & India)" obtains the largest number of "5". Overall, as expected, the United States seems to collect the largest preferences of the respondent firms ("3", "4", and "5"). The EU markets have a pattern similar to that of the United States but with more firms with lower interest. It is noteworthy that two firms in the sample

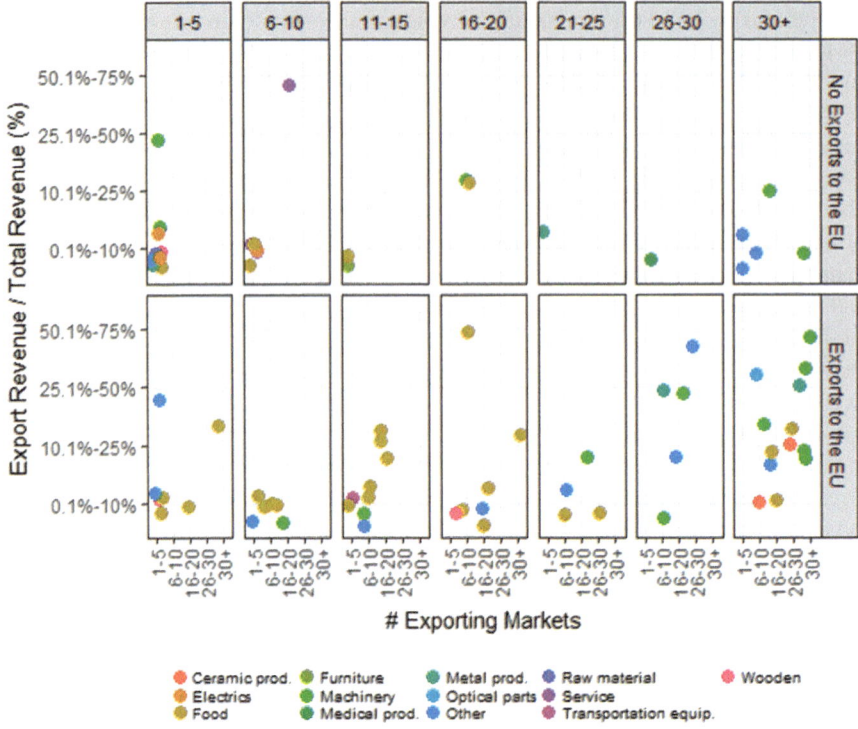

Fig. 6.2 Internationalization of respondent firms by exporting years and number of markets

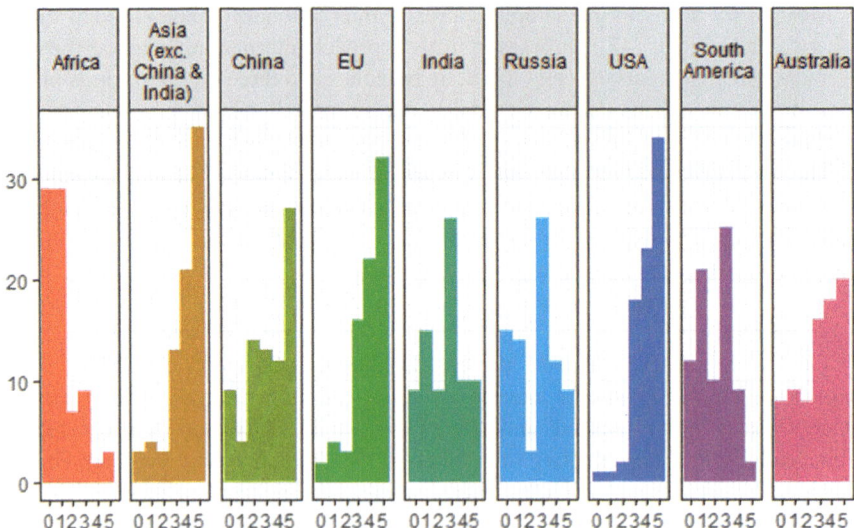

Fig. 6.3 Preferences of respondent firms in world markets

answered that they are not interested in the EU markets. China's market is well-positioned among the preferences of the respondent firms but, quite unexpectedly, more firms (9) answered that they are not interested in the Chinese market. These four markets received the largest preferences of the respondent firms. This is expected given the proximity of the Asian and Chinese markets to Japan and the importance of the American and European markets in terms of development and consumption. The Australian market is well-positioned among the preferences of the respondent firms even though the number of firms with no interest or low interest is larger. Markets like India, Russia, and South America receive more median preferences ("3"). However, Indian and Russian markets received more strong preferences than South American market. Finally, only three respondent firms have a strong interest in the African markets while more than half of the sample (58) do not have any interest or have very low interest in it.

As mentioned above, the sample includes 51 firms that export to the EU markets and 28 firms that do not. Among the firms that export to the EU, 15 firms had been exporting for a period between 1 and 5 years, 12 firms between 6 and 10 years, seven firms between 11 and 15 years, seven firms between 16 and 20 years, four firms between 21 and 25 years, one firm between 26 and 30 years, and five firms for more than 30 years.

Most of the respondent firms export to only a few EU members. In particular, 15 firms export to only one EU member, nine firms to two EU members, and eight firms to three EU members. Only five firms answered that they export to ten or more EU members. Figure 6.4 shows the destinations in Europe of the respondent firms. It emerges that the largest EU countries are the main destinations, as expected. France is the main destination of the respondent firms (34 firms), followed by Germany (23

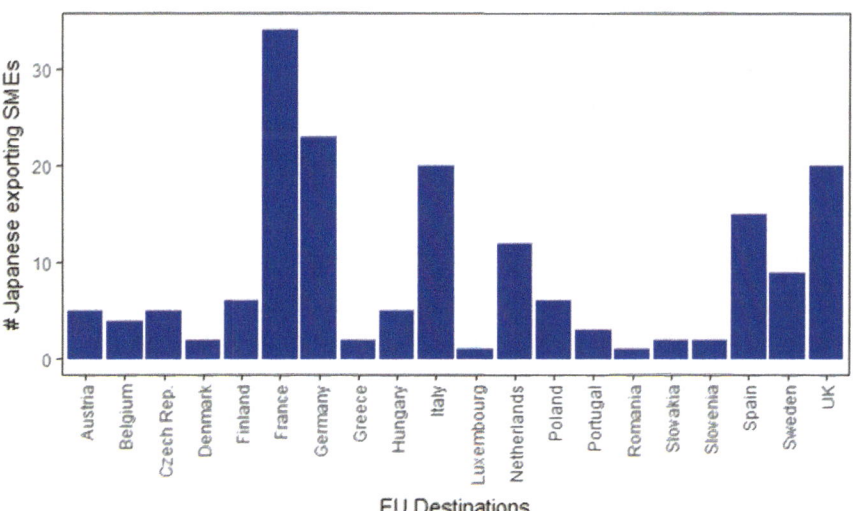

Fig. 6.4 EU destination markets of respondent firms

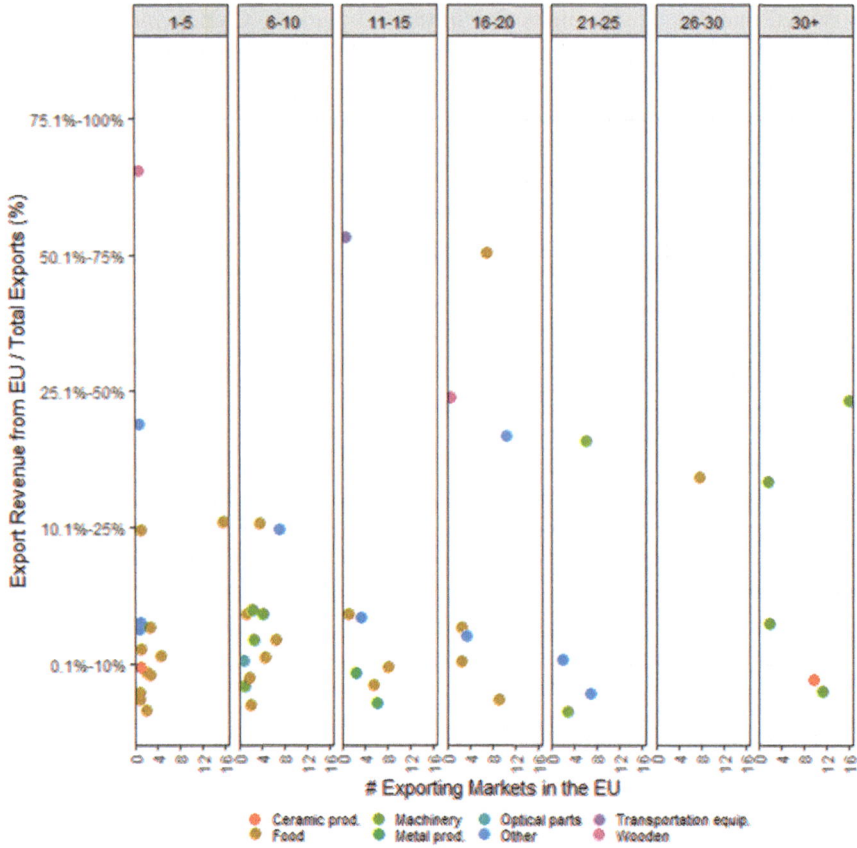

Fig. 6.5 Incidence of exports to the EU by exporting years and sectors

firms), Italy and the UK (20 firms), and Spain (15 firms). Among the Central and East European members, Poland (6 firms), Czech Republic and Hungary (5 firms each) emerge as the main destinations.[4]

Figure 6.5 shows the importance of the revenue from exports to the EU over total revenues from exports. For most of the respondent firms (37), exports to the EU account for a maximum 10% of total exports. Six firms answered that the revenue from exports to the EU accounts for 10–25% of total exports and five firms answered that this revenue accounts for between 25–50%. Only three firms of the sample stated that the EU markets account for a large weight on their total exports. In particular, two firms answered that this revenue accounts for between 50–75% and one firm answered that it accounts for more than 75% of total exports.

---

[4]It was optional for the firms to disclose the export markets. Consequently, not all the respondent firms have revealed their destination markets in the EU.

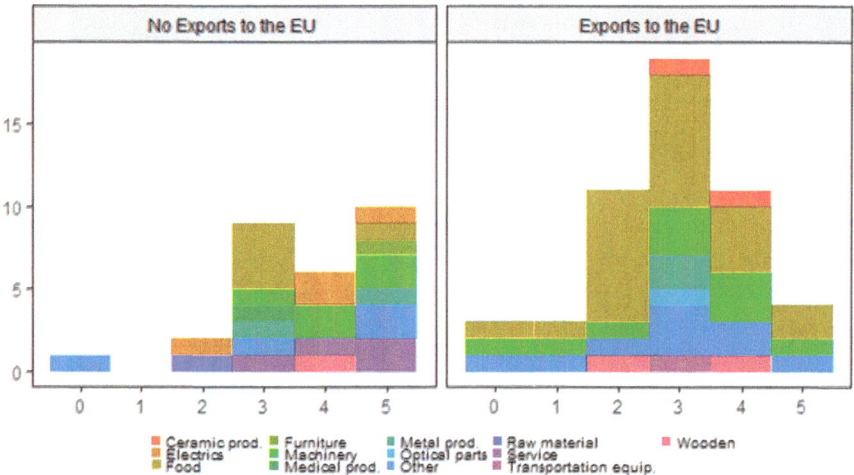

Fig. 6.6 EU market access evaluation by respondent firms

Most of the respondent firms approach the European markets through agents (35) and direct sales (32). Ten firms answered that they approach the EU markets through "other" methods as well. Only four firms answered that they had set up a branch in the EU through a 100% investment.

From these responses, we can infer that for Japanese SMEs the EU markets still account for a small proportion of their total revenue. At the same time, these markets represent an opportunity for Japanese SMEs to grow and become more internationalized. Mainly, they could achieve growth on the European markets by increasing the number of destinations (extensive strategies), and/or by focusing on expanding market share in the country where they currently export (intensive strategies).

With the following responses, we analyse what factors represent the main obstacles to exporting to the EU. We group the answers into firms that export to the EU and those that do not. Figure 6.6 shows the overall assessment of the ease to access to the EU markets, where 0 means "very easy" and 5 "very difficult". If we compare the answers from firms that export and those that do not, it results that the latter found the EU markets more difficult to access than the former. Six firms that export to the EU answered that the EU markets are easy to access, while for only four firms it is very difficult to access. Most of the Japanese SMEs that export to the EU find an average difficulty to access it.

In the following, we try to identify what measures represent the main obstacle to the export of the Japanese SMEs to the EU markets. Figure 6.7 shows that for the firms that export to the EU, the tariff barrier represents the main obstacle. These answers differ from those of firms that do not export to the EU, which place a greater emphasis on "conformity assessment", "quality control measure", and "intellectual property rights" as the main obstacles.

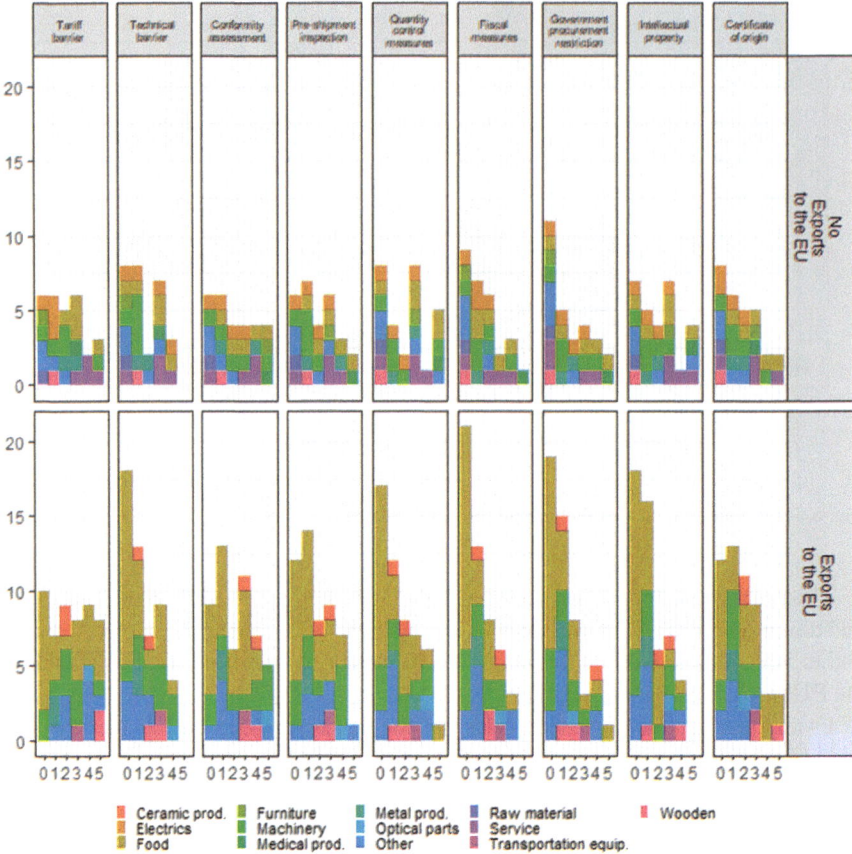

Fig. 6.7 Evaluation of tariff barrier and NTMs to the EU markets by respondent firms

Tariff barriers and NTMs will be handled by the EU–Japan EPA. Consequently, we asked Japanese SMEs whether they think the EU–Japan EPA will contribute to increasing their exports to the EU. Forty-six respondent firms answered that they think the EU–Japan EPA will not help their exports while 33 firms think it will. If we group the answers by firms that export and those that do not, we find that, among firms that do not export to the EU, 20 (71.4%) firms think that the EU–Japan EPA will not contribute, while 8 (28.6%) firms think it will. On the other hand, among firms that export to the EU, 26 (51%) firms think that the EU–Japan EPA will not help, while 25 (49%) firms think it will. Therefore, the Japanese SMEs that already export to the EU are more inclined to think that an EU–Japan EPA will help their exports to increase to the EU than Japanese SMEs that currently do not export to the EU.

However, when respondent firms answered whether they preferred an earlier implementation of the EU–Japan EPA, 55 firms answered positively while only 24 firms answered negatively. If we group the answers by firms that export and those that do not export to the EU, we find that, among firms that do not export to the EU, 10 firms (35.7%) answered negatively while 18 firms (64.3%) preferred an earlier implementation. On the other hand, among firms that export to the EU, 14 firms (27.4%) answered negatively while 37 firms (72.5%) preferred an earlier implementation. Even though most of the respondent firms do not think that the EU–Japan EPA will help their exports to increase on the EU markets, most of them would have preferred an earlier implementation. This could imply the preferences of the firms for an easier framework to export, which is favoured by the application of EPAs.

The following responses try to figure out whether the implementation of the EU–Japan EPA affects Japanese SMEs' strategy for the EU markets. Eighteen firms answered that they plan to export to new EU markets, 17 firms answered that they plan to expand the range of products on the EU markets, 11 firms answered that they would directly export from Japan, two firms plan to set up a plant in the EU, 20 firms answered that they would not change strategy while 29 firms answered that they do know yet. We group these answers in "Strategy for the EU due to the EPA" if the firms answered that they plan to expand range of product and/or export to new EU markets and/or set up plant in the EU and/or direct exports to the EU because of the EU–Japan EPA, and in "No Strategy for the EU due to the EPA" if they answered they will not change strategy or they do not know. Figures 6.8 and 6.9 show the answers of the respondent firms to the questions about the effects of the EU–Japan EPA on their exports to the EU and about an earlier implementation of the EU–Japan EPA, respectively, grouped by whether they export to the EU or they do not and whether they will change their strategy for the EU markets or they will not.

Finally, we investigate whether Japanese SMEs think that the EU–Korea FTA gave an advantage to Korean firms on the European markets. Most firms (56) answered that "they do not know" or that they do not think the question is related to their business. Twenty-one firms answered that they do not think it gave an advantage because "Korean firms are not my competitors" (15 firms) and because "the quality of our goods is superior" (6 firms). Only two firms think that the EU–Korea FTA gave an advantage to Korean firms. The fact that most firms answered that "they do not know" it is indeed quite expected. In fact, SMEs tend to have less in-depth knowledge of exporting markets, including their competitors.

6.4   Conclusion

The analysis of the responses to the survey shows that Japanese exporting SMEs have a low degree of internationalization. Revenues from the domestic market account for most of their revenues. Japan provides different programs to support the overseas expansion of SMEs such as the "Program for supporting overseas expansion by SMEs and micro businesses" and the "JAPAN Brand Development Assistance Program".

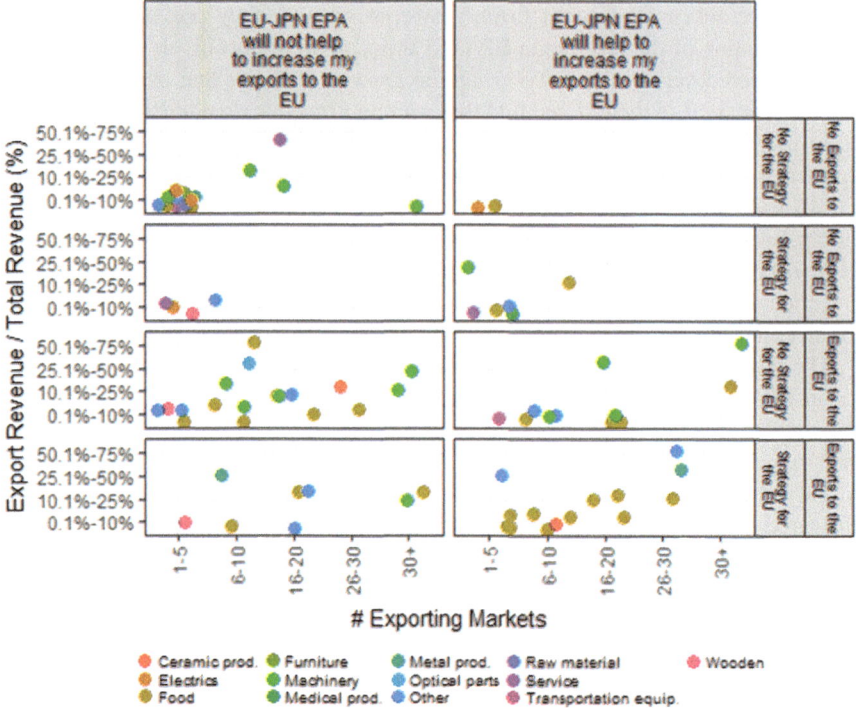

Fig. 6.8 Respondent firms' opinion about the effects of the EU–Japan EPA on their exports to the EU

EPAs also play a role in supporting the overseas expansion of firms by eliminating the import tariff and reducing the negative impact of NTMs to access the partner's market.

In addition, from the responses to the survey we can infer that, for Japanese SMEs that export to the EU, the EU markets still account for a small proportion of their total revenue. Therefore, these markets represent an opportunity for Japanese SMEs to grow and become more internationalized. Mainly, they could achieve growth on the European markets by increasing the number of destinations (extensive strategies), and/or by focusing on expanding market share in the countries where they currently export (intensive strategies).

In this context, the EU–Japan EPA may contribute to the expansion of the Japanese SMEs in the EU by easing the access to its markets. With this regard, 46 (58%) SMEs responded to the survey that they think the EU–Japan EPA would not contribute to increasing their exports to the EU while 33 (42%) firms think it would. This share increases to 49% among firms that already export to the EU. Interestingly, 70% of the firms answered that they would have preferred an earlier implementation of the EU–Japan EPA. This share slightly increases to 73% among firms that already export to the EU. Therefore, even though most of the respondent firms do not think that the

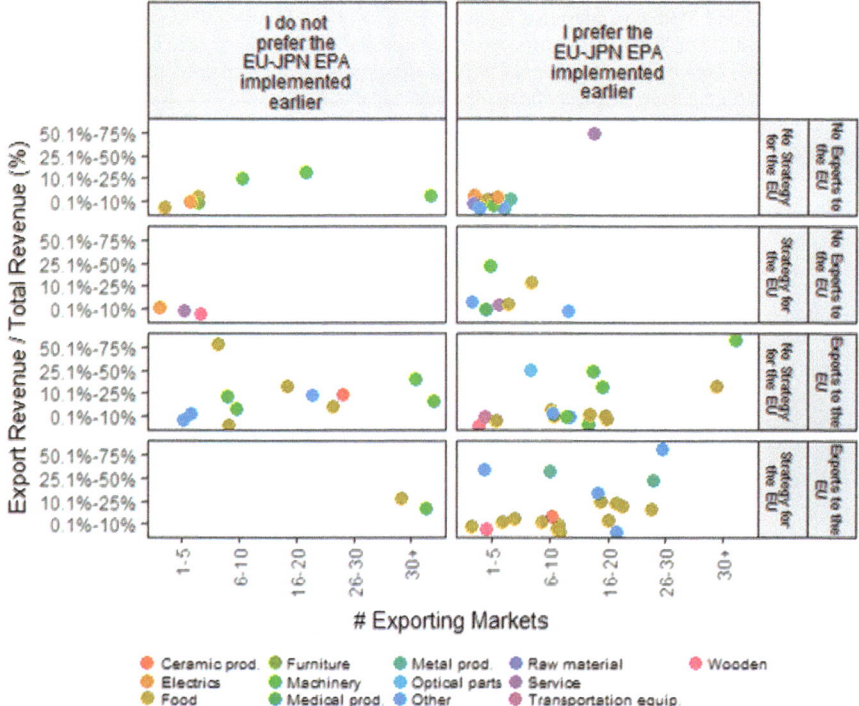

Fig. 6.9 Respondent firms' opinion about an earlier implementation of the EU–Japan EPA

EU–Japan EPA will help their exports to increase on the EU markets, most of them would have preferred an earlier implementation. This could imply the preferences of the firms for an easier framework to export, which is favoured by the application of EPAs.

References

1. Keidanren. (2007). *A call for the development and promotion of proactive external economic strategies? Toward a nation built on trade and investment, pursuing progress with Asia.* Retrieved October 16, 2007, from https://www.keidanren.or.jp/english/policy/2007/081.html
2. Keidanren. (2011). *Proposals for Japan's trade strategy.* Retrieved April 11, 2011, from https://www.keidanren.or.jp/english/policy/2011/030/proposal.html
3. Keidanren. (2012). *Chairman calls on European leaders to start negotiations on an EU-Japan FTA/EPA.* Retrieved from https://www.keidanren.or.jp/en/policy/2012/026.html
4. The Small and Medium Enterprise Agency (SMEA) of the Ministry of Economy Trade and Industry. (1999). *Small and medium-sized enterprise basic act* (Act No. 154 of 1963: Amended on December 3, 1999). Retrieved from https://www.chusho.meti.go.jp/sme_english/outline/08/01.html

5. The Small and Medium Enterprise Agency (SMEA) of the Ministry of Economy Trade and Industry (METI). (2018). *2018 white paper on small and medium enterprises in Japan: Strength to overcome Labor Shortage: The key to increasing productivity*. Retrieved from https://www.chusho.meti.go.jp/sme_english/whitepaper/whitepaper.html

Correction to: An Economic Analysis of Korea–EU FTA and Japan–EU EPA

Masahiko Yoshii and Chae-Deug Yi

Correction to:
M. Yoshii and C.-D. Yi (eds.),
An Economic Analysis of Korea–EU FTA and Japan–EU
EPA, **Kobe University Monograph Series in Social Science**
Research, https://doi.org/10.1007/978-981-33-6145-4

The original version of this book was inadvertently published with incorrect author affiliation in the book: Co-volume editor "Chae-Deug Yi" affiliation has been corrected from "Democratic People's Republic of Korea" to "Republic of Korea".

And

In the Chapter 3 belated corrections has been updated. Author names before the numbers preceding in-text bibliographical citations have been reinserted. The same has been corrected.

The chapter and book have been updated with the changes.

The updated version of the book can be found at
https://doi.org/10.1007/978-981-33-6145-4_3
https://doi.org/10.1007/978-981-33-6145-4

Printed by Books on Demand, Germany